A War on All Fronts Revisited: 2005 - 2020

A War on All Fronts Revisited: 2005 - 2020

By
Anthony Johnson

E-BookTime, LLC
Montgomery, Alabama

A War on All Fronts Revisited: 2005 - 2020

ISBN: 978-1-60862-796-7

First Edition
Published September 2020
E-BookTime, LLC
6598 Pumpkin Road
Montgomery, AL 36108
www.e-booktime.com

Acknowledgements

God: my Rock and my Salvation

Cheyenne and Gabriel: My loves, My joys, My universe.

Mom (Evelyn Johnson) and Dad (Charles Wade, Jr.): Thank you for your unconditional love, support and sacrifices. You never stopped believing in me. I love you.

Ms. Elizabeth Jones (Ma Liz): Love you and miss you.

Dr. Bernhardt Blumenthal and Gregory "Suavey G" Pearson: Love you! RIP.

My siblings (Breeland, Denise, Kim and Vernell): I love you and thank you.

The Beta Family: Erica Bryant, Vaughn Smith, Mike Jones and Eric Singleton. My love for you is deathless! It binds me with omnipotent cables. Beta Family Forever!

Leon "Ice Cube" Jones: Our brotherhood was cemented as children. You are the most honest and authentic person I've had the honor of knowing. Thank you for your friendship and counsel.

Leona Larregui, Yvette Barnes and Latioshia Jones: Love you, sisters.

Tracey Gallashaw: You are a beacon to the world.

Derrick Hill, Andre Whitherspoon, Tom Gallashaw, Moses White, Rodney McClary and Lee Parsons: I've learned so much from each one of you and because of your loyalty and wisdom...I'm a better man. Thank you, Brothers

Kamau Bright, Theodore Horne, Chad Lassiter, Craig Stroman, Terrell Bagby and Darin Toliver: Thank you, leaders of courage and integrity. The world illuminates brighter with you in it.

Tara Chestnut, Pamela and Andre Jones and Keya Pitts: Your unflinching friendship and support for more than twenty-five years has been a true blessing. CU FOREVER!

Terri Wilmott: Thank you for your support and political expertise over the years.

Tim Valentine: Thank you for your friendship and technological support.

Dr. Veronie Lawrence: Thank you for being an amazing friend and community leader. You're amazing!

Dr. Kevin Aiken: Thank you for your compassion, brilliance and leadership. You're a man of great integrity.

North 30th Street & West Lehigh Avenue (North Philadelphia): My country! The man that I've become was forged in this community.

Contents

Introduction

As a child my parents explained to me and my siblings that beyond the community where we resided there was the real world. A world where cruelty, racism and hate rules. So they prepared us. Still, they knew that their children would experience racism first hand so preparing us was essential. It didn't take long before I came face to face with racism, hate and the stereotypical views of young black boys. In 1984, four black youth in the 8th grade (Attending E. Washington Rhodes Middle School) coming home one rainy night on Roosevelt Blvd (Philadelphia) was stopped by two police officers. They jumped out of their car with guns pointing at the young men. They said, "Don't move." They lined the young men up and shortly after they removed a white woman from out of the back seat of the squad car. She's crying and completely distraught. The police officer asked her, "Was it them?" She looked at them closely, intensely and angrily. Then she said, "No. It's not them. They didn't rob me." One of the police officers was agitated and said. "Look at them again and take your time." She angrily turned to the officer and yelled, "It's not them!" He tells her to look again but she returned to the squad car. The police officer looked at me and my three friends like he wanted to hurt us. The look of disappointment on his face that we were not the ones that robbed the woman told the entire story. He angrily said to us, "Get your asses home." They say that time heals all wounds. I'm fifty-one years old! The wounds haven't healed

– and never will. What I realized that night was the laws that were created then and now are not for people of color. So now we fight a battle on two fronts. And every first-year history student know that from Alexander the Great, Napoleon and Hitler, one cannot win a war fighting on two fronts.

The other battle that African Americans face in our community is the high rate of illiteracy, unemployment and poverty that has increased violence in those communities. We must also keep in mind the mental strain it places on the residents. For example, in African American communities, mental health issues are often compounded by the psychological stress of systemic racism. As a result, African American adults are 20% more likely to report serious psychological distress than white adults. What's more, seeking mental health care is stigmatized within many black communities and just 1 in 3 African Americans who struggle with mental health issues will ever receive appropriate treatment. Therefore, the increased homicide rate inflicted on black teens and young adults' mental health is a national crisis. Yet, it is all often ignored outside of the black communities being affected. More than 85% of black homicide victims are shot and killed with guns. These facts are both appalling and unacceptable. The statistics are deeply troubling:

- Of the 7,756 black homicide victims, 6,748 (87%) were male, 1,003 (13%) were female, and five were of unknown sex (less than 1%).
- The homicide rate for black male victims was 37.12 per 100, 000. In comparison, the overall rate for male homicide victims was 8.29 per 100,000.
- The homicide rate for female black victims was 5.07 per 100,000. In comparison, the overall rate for female homicide victims was 1.97 per 100,000.

- 501 black homicide victims (7%) were less than 18 years old and 146 black homicide victims (2%) were 65 years of age or older. The average age was 31 years old.
- For homicides in which the weapon used could be identified, 87% of black victims (6,505 out of 7,442) were shot and killed with guns. Of these, 66% (4,319 victims) were killed with handguns. There were 540 victims killed with knives or other cutting instruments, 193 victims killed by bodily force, and 117 victims killed by a blunt object.

Contrary to what the media and the general population believe African Americans show the highest levels of anger and shame after reading about black-on-black crime. African Americans in the United States are disproportionately affected by homicide. From 2016 thru 2020, African Americans represented 13% of the nation's population, yet accounts for 57% of all homicide victims. An important part of ending our nation's gun violence epidemic will involve reducing homicides in the African American community.

In addition, individuals living in communities where violence is prevalent are at increased risk for a broad range of negative health and behavior outcomes. An increased understanding of how trauma resulting from community violence influences development, health, and behavior can lead to improvements in the way many social services are delivered as well as policy changes at the local and federal levels. For African Americans victims of homicide; like all victims of homicide, handguns are far and away the number one murder tool.

While the majority of Americans report that they believe Chicago is the most dangerous city in America, looking solely at the murder rate per capita, Philadelphia could be considered one of the most dangerous big cities in America with a murder rate of 21.5 per 100,000 people. The majority of Americans ranked Philadelphia middle of the road in terms of considering it safe. 48% of Americans consider Philadelphia either very safe or fairly safe. The city of Brotherly Love also boasts an assault and robbery rate of more than 500 per 100,000 people. The 303 homicides in the city in December during 2019 represent a 7% increase compared to the same time in 2018 and the highest figure since 344 in 2007.

Successful efforts to reduce America's black homicide toll, like America's homicide toll as a whole, must put a focus on reducing access and exposure to firearms. An important part of ending the gun violence epidemic is to reduce homicides in the African American community once and for all.

I.

Black and Living in America

Racial violence and racial health inequities in the midst of the COVID-19 pandemic disproportionately impact on African Americans. The murders of George Floyd, Breonna Taylor and Jacob Blake shot seven times by an officer in Kenosha, Wisconsin is just another example of a longstanding history of racial terror and police brutality against black people in America, and has sparked global outrage. While these acts of violence is horrific in its own right, its occurrence against the backdrop of a global pandemic that has wreaked havoc in black communities – causing over 30,000 deaths within the span of 4 months – has forced a collective reckoning with the fact that racism, in all of its forms, is deadly and has a devastating impact on black lives.

Due to a reckless and uncoordinated federal response, America remains the global epicenter of the COVID-19 pandemic with over 6 million confirmed cases and more that 180,000 confirmed deaths. Black people and other marginalized racial groups are shouldering a disproportionate burden in the current pandemic. Blacks comprise 13% of the US population but roughly one quarter of COVID-19 deaths and are nearly four times more likely to die from COVID-19 compared to whites (94·2 vs 24·8 deaths per 100,000). Black people across all age groups are nearly three times more likely than white people to contract COVID-19. These numbers, while striking, are not surprising and mirror well-documented patterns of morbidity and mortality across a wide range of health outcomes that have been observed in the USA for decades. Experts contend that "racism and not race" is the primary driver of these inequities with many citing "interlocking systems of racism" that have converged to increase exposure, transmission, and death among African American. These systems – from healthcare to housing for example, are all rooted in an ideology of white supremacy and the institution of slavery that dates back over 400 years and are maintained by racist policies and practices that construct and reinforce inequitable access to power and resources.

For example, racialized economic exploitation vis-à-vis racial capitalism has been cited as a major driver of increased risk of infection among Blacks. According to data from the US census, 43% of Black and Latino workers (compared with 25% of white workers) are employed in service or production jobs that have been deemed "essential" during the pandemic.

Since 2005, African Americans have made great strides including the election of America's first African American president. We've seen a rise of more African Americans becoming CEO's of Fortune 500 companies although, it shouldn't have taken this long. Black people have a great deal to be proud of since the start of the 21st century. And yet, fast forward to 2020, African Americans are in the cross hair to an increasing volatile America trying to hit the reset button of an America that African Americans and other people of color have no desire of returning to.

In 2016, 63 million Americans elected Donald Trump, whose campaign slogan of "Making America Great Again" was the dog whistle of blatant racism and bigotry. During the contentious election between Trump and Secretary Hillary Clinton, (who won the popular vote by more than three million votes) Trump's campaign appearances was enthusiastically reported by the media filled with intolerance, violence, racism, xenophobia and misogyny. He used racism as a weapon and in so doing defied all the odds and defeated Hillary Clinton.

Since his presidency, Trump has failed to assist Puerto Rico during the worst hurricane in the country's history. He followed that up by calling Haiti a "Shit hole" country and tossing undocumented children in cages. He has awakened the racial intolerance and hatred within Americans that laid dormant for 50 years although we began seeing it unfold with the election of Barack Obama in 2008. Since, *A War On All Fronts* was released in 2005, America has had a surge in terror attacks – by Americans. There have been more terrorists' attacks perpetrated by Americans against Americans in the last decade than at any other time. We no longer worry about foreign terrorists. It is the American terrorists that we must be concerned with.

America's judicial system and law enforcement continues to be an incessant adversary to black people. Since 2005, Sandra Bland, Tamir Rice, Trayvon Martin, Mike Brown, Philando Castile, Freddy Gray, Sam Dubose, Alton Sterling, Walter Scott and Eric Garner and now with the murder of George Floyd from Minneapolis are just a few that police officer(s) and non-law enforcement agents (Zimmerman) murdered and were exonerated by the judicial system. African Americans and other people of color; men, women and children now face an America of being arrested or murdered for walking, singing, dancing, living in their own homes/ apartments, playing with a toy gun, selling CD's, cigarettes, water and/or lemonade. Furthermore, they are murdered for wearing a hoodie, sitting in a car with friends playing music while respecting law enforcement. According to the NAACP Criminal Justice data, racial disparities for incarceration continue to increase:

- Between 2005 thru 2018, the number of people incarcerated in America increased from roughly 200,000 to over 1.8 million.
- In 2018, African Americans constituted 2.5 million, or 34%, of the total 6.8 million correctional populations.
- African Americans are incarcerated at more than five times the rate of whites.
- The imprisonment rate for African American women is twice that of white women.
- Nationwide, African American children represent 32% of children who are arrested.
- Though African Americans and Hispanics make up approximately 32% of the US population, they comprised 60% of all incarcerated people in 2018.

According to the Washington Post, (December 2015) there was a disproportionate number of black victims in fatal traffic stops:

- ➢ 1 in 3 are African American, making the roadside interaction one of the most common precursors to a fatal police shooting for people from 2015.
- ➢ Black people accounted for a disproportionate share of traffic stop deaths, a finding that experts on policing said provides fresh evidence that blacks are pulled over more frequently than other drivers.
- ➢ Justice Department investigations of local and state police agencies have repeatedly found evidence of

racial disparities in traffic enforcement. In 2014, the Justice Department released a national survey showing that black drivers were significantly more likely than whites to have been pulled over in the previous 12 months.

Depending on one's level of understanding and awareness about the plight of black and brown people, one might argue that they are better off today than they were 50 years ago, especially when one remembers Jim Crow; an era during which black people were ruthlessly brutalized, particularly by white supremacist groups such as the Ku Klux Kan. However, if one constructively analyzed the accomplishment gap between students of color and their white counterparts, the decline in incomes, and other forms of educational and socioeconomic inequality that black people, particularly poor students of color, have been experiencing over the last several decades, one would realize that substantially; nothing has changed.

Structural racism operates at the societal level and is the power used by the dominant group to provide members of the group with advantages, while disadvantaging the non-dominant group. The dominant group uses structural racism not only to obtain resources, such as employment and wages, but also to limit the non-dominant group's access to these resources. During the Jim Crow era, structural racism sponsored by the federal and state governments explicitly created advantages for whites and disadvantages for African Americans. Structural racism still exists after the Jim Crow era, which significantly disadvantages minority women and limits their access to health care. The unemployment rate for African Americans has been at least twice as high as white people unemployment for all but seven years during the 53-year period between 1962 and 2015. Research shows that more than one-third of jobs are filled through referrals, which has not changed for the last 26 years. African American women with some college get paid $15.58 an hour compared to $22.51 an hour for white men with some college. In fact, African American women with some college get paid only $0.42 more an hour than Caucasian men without a high school diploma. African American women with an advanced degree, such as a master's degree, make $7 less per hour than white men with a bachelor's degree and $17 less per hour than white men with an advanced degree.

In terms of annual pay, African American women with a bachelor's degree or more make $50,200, about the same as a white man with some college.

A Caucasian man with a bachelor's degree or more makes $76,708 annually, almost $27,000 more than an African American woman with a bachelor's degree or more.

African American women with a bachelor's degree make $46,000 annually, only $3,500 more than a Caucasian male with only a high school diploma. African American women with a master's degree make $55,843, compared to $86,330 for white men with a master's degree. Overall, African American women would have had to work seven months into 2017 to be paid the same as Caucasian men in 2016.

African American families have a fraction of the wealth of white families, leaving them more economically insecure and with far fewer opportunities for economic mobility. Even after considering positive factors such as increased education levels, African Americans have less wealth than whites. Less wealth translates into fewer opportunities for upward mobility and is compounded by lower income levels and fewer chances to build wealth or pass accumulated wealth down to future generations.

Several key factors exacerbate this vicious cycle of wealth inequality. Black households, for example, have far less access to tax-advantaged forms of savings, due in part to a long history of employment discrimination and other discriminatory practices. A well-documented history of mortgage market discrimination means that blacks are significantly less likely to be homeowners than whites which mean they have less access to the savings and tax benefits that come with owning a home. Thus, African Americans have less access to stable jobs, good wages, and retirement benefits at work – all key drivers by which American families gain access to savings. Moreover, under the current tax code, families with higher incomes receive increased tax incentives associated with both housing and retirement savings. Because African Americans tend to have lower incomes, they inevitably receive fewer tax benefits even if they are homeowners or have retirement savings accounts. The bottom line is that persistent housing and labor market discrimination and segregation worsen the damaging cycle of wealth inequality.

Now burning black people while still alive or cutting off their genitals or attending public lynchings of which "picnics" were created as a result may be from America's long, wretched past of enslavement and genocide but there have been new initiatives to keep African Americans and other people of color downtrodden. Mass incarceration of people of color is the 21st century version of slavery. Can we, the people of America; Black, White, Asian, Native American and Latino work together and have an open and candid conversation about structural racism? Can we finally address the social, political and racial dichotomy that's destroying America? Or do we continue pretending that America is great for everyone?

The senseless murders of African Americans and the devastating impact of the COVID-19 have brought into sharp focus the deadly consequences of racism in the US and beyond. Since June 2020, anti-racist protests such as the Black Lives Matter movement have mobilized millions of people around the world. Movements like this one that organize from the bottom up, demand a radical restructuring of our society and a re-imagined world where Black lives truly matter.

II.

A Nation Divided: The Deterioration of Race Relations in America

Amid ongoing protests over unequal treatment of black Americans and police brutality, historic unemployment and a pandemic that has disproportionately battered black communities, the conversation in this country has clearly shifted. With 42% of Americans calling race relations extremely important to their vote for president this fall, the issue now stands on par with the economy and health care near the top of campaign issues.

Among those prioritizing race relations, there's a demographic and political split. Most black voters call it extremely important: 61%. That's an increase from the 34% of black voters who said the same in 2015. Right now, 60% of Democrats and Democratic-leaning independent voters say race relations are extremely important. Compare that with just 18% of Republicans and Republican-leaners who said the same. Protests have raged in the US for months in 2020 sparked by the May 25 death of George Floyd, a black man who was killed while in police custody, as well as the recent killings of others like Breonna Taylor and Ahmaud Arbery. The nationwide spread of anti-racism protests has led to calls to defund and demilitarize police departments. The presidential election is still more than three months away and it's hard to predict whether this same conversation will continue at the current pitch through November.

A majority of Americans say race relations in the United States are bad, and of those, about seven-in-ten say things are getting even worse. Roughly two-thirds say it has become more common for people to express racist or racially insensitive views since Donald Trump was elected, even if not necessarily more acceptable. Opinions about the state of race relations, Trump's handling of the issue and the amount of attention paid to race vary considerably across racial and ethnic groups. Blacks, Hispanics and Asians are more likely than whites to say Trump has made race relations worse and that there's too little attention paid to race in the U.S. these days. In addition, large majorities of blacks, Hispanics and Asians say people not seeing discrimination where it exists is a bigger problem in the U.S. than people seeing it where it doesn't exist, but whites are about evenly divided on this.

More than two years into the Trump administration, a plurality of Americans think racism in the United States is getting worse, according to a poll conducted by the Washington Post in 2015 But a significant number still don't think it is a major problem – at least not a problem they care to discuss. As each week brings more news stories about race relations, large percentages of Americans are realizing that issues that some thought had been settled decades ago are still very much alive.

The NBC News and Survey Monkey poll released the same week that ABC canceled its "Roseanne" reboot in 2018; this after its star, Roseanne Barr, tweeted racist comments about Valerie Jarret, former advisor to Barack Obama revealed in her book that the former president's vision of America was shaken by Donald Trump's election and a Harvard study that dramatically increased the death toll linked to Hurricane Maria, raised questions about whether the Trump administration's handling of the disaster in Puerto Rico had racial undertones.

While much attention is being paid in 2020 to the strides that have been made 50 years since President Lyndon B. Johnson green lit the Kerner Commission to study race in the United States, the majority of Americans – more than 6 in 10 said racism remains a major problem in our society. And more people chose race over religion, gender and class as the biggest cause of division, according to the poll by the Washington Post in 2015. One finding in the poll that's worth noting is how rarely some Americans discuss race issues. Nearly half of the respondents – 47% said race relations never or rarely come up in conversations with family and friends. This means that while the majority of Americans think race relations are worsening, far fewer are discussing it with the people closest to them. It's hard to imagine being able to work toward a solution to a problem that a large percentage of people won't even discuss.

According to Reuters, (2017) as Trump neared his 100th day in the White House after a campaign punctuated by his inflammatory comments about Muslims and immigrants, a number of Americans say U.S. race relations are deteriorating. The poll, taken from March 28, 2017 to April 3, 2017 asked more than 2,800 adults to rate the danger of racism and bigotry in America. About 36% gave it the worst rating possible, saying they considered racism and bigotry an *imminent threat* to the country. That is up a few points from the 29% who answered the same way in 2015. 1 in 4 Americans surveyed in the Reuters-Ipsos poll said *people in their community get along worse than before.* Highly publicized police shootings of African Americans has only strained community bonds further. So the deadly mass killings in Orlando and San Bernardino, California, by assailants inspired at least in part by Islamic extremist groups. Some Trump critics say he continues to stoke the enmity with his incendiary campaign rhetoric, including vows to ban Muslim visitors and deport millions of undocumented immigrants.

According to civil rights groups including the Southern Poverty Law Center and Anti-Defamation League reported a sharp uptick in incidents targeting minorities after Trump's election. Some of Trump supporters have said he has made efforts to close the divide.

In a post-election television interview in November (2017) Trump said he was saddened by acts of bigotry done in his name and called on perpetrators to "Stop it" (Reuters 2017). As president, he invited the Congressional Black Caucus and heads of historically black colleges to the White House. He also condemned anti-Semitic violence. However, critics believed inviting Congressional Black Caucus and heads of historically black colleges to the White House was nothing more than a photo op.

The poll found 46% of Democrats surveyed said racism and bigotry pose an imminent threat to the country, up from 35% two years ago. That figure was sharply lower for Republicans: 27% now compared to 24% in 2015. The Reuters/Ipsos poll was conducted online in English in all 50 states. Respondents answered a series of questions, including one asking them to rate their concern about racism and bigotry on a scale of 1 to 5, with 1 meaning "no threat" and 5 meaning "imminent threat." The poll gathered responses from 1,268 Democrats and 1,008 Republicans. It has a credibility interval, a measure of accuracy, of two percentage points for the entire group, three points for Democrats and four points for Republicans.

In a poll conducted by NBC in May 2018, a majority of Americans say racism remains a major problem in American society and politics, according to NBC News|SurveyMonkey poll. Overall, 64% said racism remains a major problem in our society. 30% agreed that racism exists today, but it isn't a major problem.

Would you say that racism in American society & politics...

Remains a major problem	64%
Exists today but is not a major problem	30
Once existed but no longer exists	3
Never been a major problem	1

Data: NBC News/SurveyMonkey poll May 14-21, 2018

The poll coincided with an MSNBC town hall meeting titled, *Everyday Racism in America*, where hosts Joy Ann Reid and Chris Hayes addressed the complex issue of racial bias in America and what can be done to address it. The town hall took place in Philadelphia, where two black men were arrested while waiting for someone in a Starbucks, prompting days of protests and accusations of racism against the coffee chain, and on the same day the chain closed 8,000 stores nation-wide for racial bias training. The Starbucks arrests were just one in a string of high-profile episodes involving minorities who appeared to have been racially profiled while doing something innocuous – sitting in a coffee shop, barbecuing in a park, or taking a nap in a Yale common room. These incidents which caught fire on social media, had set off a wave of protests and prompted a national conversation about facing racism in everyday life.

Pluralities of Americans said race relations in the United States is getting worse (45%) and think that too little attention is paid to race and racial issues (41%). Overall, a 30% plurality think race is the biggest source of division in America today, up from 26% in February (2018). Racial tensions can be tied to large national events, but the poll also finds stark differences by race focused on everyday experiences. 4 in 10 African Americans say they have been treated unfairly in a store or restaurant because of their race compared to a quarter of Hispanics and only 7% of whites.

Treated unfairly in a store or restaurant based on your race?

	All adults	White	Black	Hispanic
Yes, treated unfairly	15%	7%	40%	26%
No, not treated unfairly	82	90	57	70

Data: NBC News/SurveyMonkey poll, May 14-21, 2018

In early 2018, three black Airbnb guests in Southern California were detained after a white neighbor called the police. About a week later, a white Yale University student called the police when she found a black student napping in the common room of their dorm. In February 2018, the restaurant chain Applebee's apologized and fired three employees for their involvement in racially profiling two African American customers, falsely accusing them of not paying their check. A video of the incident went viral, prompting the apology. In April 2018, another viral video showed two black men in Philadelphia being arrested after Starbucks employees called 911 to say the men were trespassing. The company apologized and then closed all stores for the afternoon on May 29 for racial sensitivity training. Also in May 2018, a video of a white woman who called the police on a black family barbecuing by a lake in Oakland, California went viral.

Other incidents in 2018 include ordinary citizens being harassed or questioned for speaking Spanish, such as the Manhattan attorney who berated restaurant employees on camera for speaking the language and threatening to call immigration authorities and the Border Patrol agent who detained two women for speaking Spanish at a Montana gas station. Racial discrimination isn't just felt in public spaces. Just under a quarter of Americans said they have experienced discrimination in the workplace based on their race but African Americans are more likely than any other racial subgroup to experience it. About half (48%) of African-Americans said they've experienced workplace discrimination based on their race compared to 36% of Hispanics and only 14% of whites.

Experienced discrimination in workplace based on your race?

	All adults	White	Black	Hispanic
Yes	23%	14%	48%	36%
No	63	72	43	52
Not employed	10	12	6	8

Data, NBC News/SurveyMonkey poll, May 14-21, 2018

There are further divides among racial subgroups when asked specifically about how each race is perceived in society. A whopping 72% of Americans think that racial discrimination against blacks is a serious problem in this country, while 89% of African Americans and 81% of Hispanics share that sentiment, 68% of whites said it's a serious problem and 30% said it's not a serious problem.

Overall, a majority think white people benefit from advantages in society that black people do not have. Among African Americans, 84% said white people benefit a great deal or fair amount. Among Hispanics, 71% said white people benefit and 25% said they do not. But half of white people said they don't enjoy any advantages, as compared to 47% of white people who said they did.

Whites benefit from societal advantages that blacks do not?

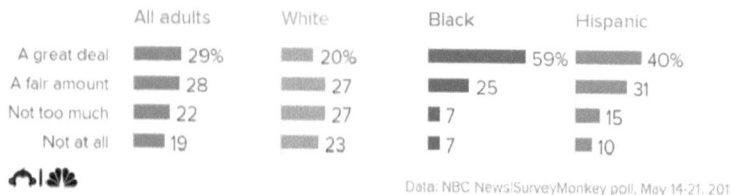

	All adults	White	Black	Hispanic
A great deal	29%	20%	59%	40%
A fair amount	28	27	25	31
Not too much	22	27	7	15
Not at all	19	23	7	10

Data: NBC News/SurveyMonkey poll, May 14-21, 2018

Day to day, overwhelming majorities of African Americans (71%) and Hispanics (69%) said they interact with a mix of people from different races at work or school. A majority of whites also said they interact with a mix of different races (59%) but 20% of whites said they interact with mostly whites. Addressing racial disparities in America will not simply dissipate. We all have a role to play and must acknowledge that racism has destroyed America's judicial and societal systems. Inequality and racism not only exist in America, it is shaping the nation's policies. The time is now that we work together and address these calamities. The future of America depends on our efforts.

Protests continue across the country, and polls finds 58% of Americans disapprove of President Trump's handling of race relations, while 33% approve; along party lines with 72% of Republicans approving while 92% of Democrats disapprove. African-Americans overwhelmingly disapprove of the president's overall job performance and his handling of race relations.

At the same time, more Americans are now saying racial discrimination impacts both treatment by police and chances of getting ahead. Eight in 10 Americans feel discrimination against African-Americans exists today, including half who say there is a lot of discrimination and 31% who say there is some. News polls also found 52% believe white people have a better chance of getting ahead, up from 39% in polling conducted in 2015. At the same time, 57% of Americans now believe police are more likely to use deadly force against a black person.

A majority of both white and black people believe race relations in the U.S. are generally bad, with just 17% saying they're getting better. Forty-two percent say they're getting worse, while 39% say they're staying the same. More Americans believe the state of race relations is more negative than it was a year ago.

III.

The American Judicial System vs. Citizens of Color

In June 2020, hundreds of thousands of Americans have taken to the streets protesting police brutality against black people. More than 10,000 protesters have been arrested, many for low-level offenses such as curfew violations and failure to disperse.

Once locked up, many people must pay cash bail to be released from detention. The amount of bail is determined by the court. Research suggests racial bias against black defendants plays a part in the level of bail set by the court. At a time when jails and prisons across the U.S. have seen widespread outbreaks of coronavirus, the cash bail system poses an unnecessary health risk.

Who does the cash bail system affect most?

Almost half a million people – three-quarters of the total number of people in jails – have not been convicted of a crime. Of these, 90 percent – the poorest Americans with the fewest resources – remain incarcerated because they cannot afford bail.

The cash bail system disproportionately impacts people of color, fueling a pervasive problem of structural racism in our criminal justice system. The pretrial population is disproportionally Black and Hispanic and has more than doubled over the past 15 years. Black and Hispanic Americans are more likely to be stopped by the police and experience police violence at the time of arrest; they also are more likely to be poor and unable to raise bail funds. The cash bail system also compounds underlying health disparities in access to care that has led to worse outcomes for Blacks and Hispanics compared to white Americans.

How does the cash bail system affect health and health care systems?

Keeping people in jail if they cannot afford cash bail is bad for their health. A well-documented body of research describes the negative health outcomes associated with and amplified by incarceration. This includes higher rates of HIV, hepatitis C, and tuberculosis. Incarcerated individuals also have a higher likelihood of chronic illness like hypertension, asthma, arthritis, and cervical cancer, as well as mental health issues such as anxiety, depression, and schizophrenia. Black Americans often have disproportionately high rates of chronic and infectious diseases because of other social factors; these conditions are compounded by the impact of the prison environment, poor quality health care in correctional facilities, and the fallout after release from incarceration, such as lack of access to housing and jobs and a high rate of poverty.

Jails and localities rely on secured bail money as revenue, creating a perverse incentive for police to make arrests. However, communities pay for the consequences of pretrial incarceration in many ways. Research has found that even short pretrial detention of two to three days may have negative effects on court appearance, conviction, sentencing, and future involvement with the criminal justice system. And, despite the incoming revenue, the system is expensive. Pretrial incarceration alone costs local governments and tax-payers an estimated $13.6 billion annually. Providing health care in jails is difficult and expensive and often is paid for by other local agencies.

Policy implications

Ending cash bail. Ending the cash bail system would allow state and local policymakers to address structural racism in a significant way.

In response to the COVID-19 pandemic, California elim-inated cash bail for most low-level offenses. This allowed thousands of defendants to await trial at home rather than in crowded jails during a pandemic. Washington, D.C., New Jersey, and Harris County, Texas (i.e., including Houston, the third-largest jail system in the country) have reformed their pretrial systems by essentially ending cash bail. D.C. and New Jersey have released approximately 95 percent of defendants pretrial; nearly 90 percent of them appear at their trial dates. States and localities could eliminate cash bail for certain misdemeanors, nonviolent felonies, and other minor offenses, and explore different ways for defendants to reassure judges they will make their court appearances.

Diverting funds spent on pretrial incarceration to invest in social services. There is a clear financial case to be made for ending cash bail systems across the country – some portion of the funds could be reinvested in socials services. Invest-ing in access to health care (i.e., primary care, mental health, and addiction services), education, housing, transportation, employment services, and violence reduction at the com-munity level can help better address the social determinants of health and structural racism afflicting Black and Hispanic communities.

Longer-term reform of the criminal justice system. Ending cash bail is one way to address the entrenched racism in the U.S. criminal justice system. People of color, especially black people, committing minor traffic violations or misdemeanors are disproportionately likely to experience police violence and find themselves in jail. As the recent swell of nation-wide protests after the death of George Floyd, Breonna Taylor and others indicates, there is widespread public support for police and criminal justice reform. Such reform – starting with an end to the cash bail system – would have a positive impact on the health of many Americans of color and could help address structural racism.

A study in 2018 by the American Civil Liberties Union found that more than 3,200 people nationwide are serving life terms without parole for *nonviolent offenses*. Of those prisoners, 80% are behind bars for drug-related convictions. Sixty per-cent are African-American, 18% are white, and 16% are Latino of what the ACLU calls "extreme racial disparities." The crimes that led to life sentences include stealing gas from a truck, shoplifting, possessing a crack pipe, facili-tating a $10 sale of marijuana, and attempting to cash a stolen check.

When you consider that much of the criminal justice system was built, honed and firmly established during the Jim Crow era, an era; almost everyone, conservatives included, will concede rife with racism, this is pretty intuitive. The modern criminal justice system helped preserve racial order to keep black people in their place.

For much of the early 20th century and in some parts of the country today, that's the primary function. That it might retain some of those proclivities in 2020 shouldn't be all that surprising.

The effect of the War on Drugs on communities of color has been tragic. Sentencing disparities and selective enforcement of drug laws mean that there are more black people under the control of prison and corrections departments today than were ever enslaved by this country. Despite the fact that whites engage in drug offenses at a higher rate than African Americans do, black people are incarcerated for drug offenses at a rate that is ten times greater than that of whites.

Some progress has been made however. In 2010, Congress passed the Fair Sentencing Act (FSA), which represents a decade long, bipartisan effort to reduce the racial disparities caused by draconian crack cocaine sentencing laws and restore confidence in the criminal justice system particularly in communities of color. And in 2011, the U.S. Sentencing Commission voted to retroactively apply the new FSA guidelines to individuals sentenced before the law was enacted. This decision will help ensure that over 12,000 people – 85% of whom are African American will have the opportunity to have their sentences for crack cocaine offenses reviewed by a federal judge and possibly reduced.

Race may be the deciding factor in whether you're deemed innocent in a court of law. That's the takeaway from a study for the National Registry of Exonerations, published in 2018. Researchers Samuel Gross, Maurice Possley, and Klara Stephens analyzed years of exoneration data; looking at how race may influence whether someone is wrongfully convicted and later cleared of a crime they didn't commit. *African Americans are only 13% of the American population but a majority of innocent defendants wrongfully convicted of crimes and later exonerated*, the researchers write. They constitute 47% of the 1,900 exonerations listed in the National Registry of Exonerations, (as of October 2018) and the great majority of more than 1,800 additional innocent defendants who were framed and convicted of crimes in 15 large scale police scandals and later cleared.

Here are the results taken from the study:

How race influences convictions

Innocent black people are more likely to be wrongfully convicted of crimes than innocent white people

MURDER	SEXUAL ASSAULT	DRUG CRIMES
7 times more likely to be convicted	**3.5 times** more likely to be convicted	**12 times** more likely to be convicted

Source: National Registry of Exonerations

For murders, researchers found not just that African Americans were more likely than white people to be wrongfully convicted but that innocent black people spent more time in prison before they were exonerated. Judging from exonerations, innocent black people are about seven times more likely to be convicted of murder than innocent white people.

African Americans imprisoned for murder are more likely to be innocent if they were convicted of killing white victims.

Only about 15% of murders by African Americans have white victims, but 31% of innocent African-American murder exonerees were convicted of killing white people. The convictions that led to murder exonerations with black defendants were 22% more likely to include misconduct by police officers than those with white defendants. Exonerations of innocent murder defendants take longer if the defendant is black: 14.2 years on average, than if he is white (11.2 years). For death row exonerations in the National Registry of Exonerations the average delays and the difference by race are larger – 16 years for black defendants and 12 years for whites

There were similar findings for sexual assault:

Judging from exonerations, a black prisoner serving time for sexual assault is three times more likely to be innocent than a white sexual assault convict.

The major cause for this huge racial disparity appears to be the high danger of mistaken eyewitness identification by white victims in violent crimes with black assailants.

Assaults on white women by African American men are a small minority of all sexual assaults in the United States, but they constitute half of sexual assaults with eyewitness misidentifications that led to exoneration. African American sexual assault exonerees received much longer prison sentences than white sexual assault exonerees, and they spent on average almost four years longer in prison before exoneration. It appears that innocent black sexual assault defendants receive harsher sentences than whites if they are convicted, and then face greater resistance to exoneration even in cases in which they are ultimately released.

And much of the same was true for drug crimes:

The best national evidence on drug use shows that African Americans and whites use illegal drugs at about the same rate. Nonetheless, African Americans are about five times as likely to go to prison for drug possession as whites and judging from exonerations, innocent black people are about 12 times more likely to be convicted of drug crimes than innocent white people.

Why do police officers who conduct these outrageous programs of framing innocent drug defendants concentrate on African Americans? The simple answer: *Because that's what they do in all aspects of drug-law enforcement. Guilty or innocent, they always focus disproportionately on African Americans.* Of the many costs that America's *War on Drugs* inflicts on the black community, the practice of deliberately charging innocent defendants with fabricated crimes may be the most shameful.

Overall, the study paints a very clear picture: black people are at disadvantaged within the criminal justice system, leading to massive disparities even among those who are entirely innocent. The causes identified run from inevitable consequences of patterns in crime and punishment to deliberate acts of racism, with many stops in between. They differ sharply from one type of crime to another. For example, the researchers found that some of the disparity is driven in large part by higher murder rates in black communities. If the real criminal is black, anybody who is mistakenly convicted for that crime will almost inevitably be *African Americans* as well. But the researchers found that law enforcement misconduct and racism also played major roles, such as police deliberately targeting black people for raids, arrests, and false confessions, witnesses identifying the wrong suspect, a notoriously error-prone process when white Americans are asked to identify black strangers and preexisting racial biases among jurors and judges influencing convictions and sentences.

A caveat: The study only looked at raw data for exonerations and in some cases, the general population. The researchers stress that their data likely does not cover all innocent people in prison given that there are likely thousands of innocent people in prison who have yet to be or never will be exonerated.

And just looking at the broad raw data likely misses some nuances in some individual cases, such as how criminal histories explained differences in prison sentences or attempts to seek exoneration.

Still, the data implicates the criminal justice system as vastly racially disparate – not only prosecuting and imprisoning the innocent but doing so in large part because of their race. It is just the latest evidence that America's criminal justice system is far from fair and equal.

There are many indicators of the profound impact of disproportionate rates of incarceration in communities of color. Perhaps the most stark among these are the data generated by the U.S. Department of Justice that project that if current trends continue, 1 of every 3 black males born today will go to prison in his lifetime, as will 1 of every 6 Latino males. Regardless of what one views as the causes of this situation, it should be deeply disturbing to all Americans that these figures represent the future for a generation of children growing up today.

In order to develop policies and practices to reduce unwarranted racial disparities in the criminal justice system, it is necessary to assess the factors that have produced the current record levels of incarceration and racial/ethnic disparity. These are clearly complicated issues but four areas of analysis are key:

- Disproportionate crime rates

- Disparities in criminal justice processing

- Overlap of race and class effects

- Impact of race neutral policies

➤ **Disproportionate Crime Rates**

A series of studies conducted during the past thirty years has examined the degree to which disproportionate rates of incarceration for African Americans are related to greater involvement in crime. Examining national data for 1979, criminologist Alfred Blumstein concluded that 80% of racial disparity could be explained by greater involvement in crime, although a subsequent study reduced this figure to 76% for the 1991 prison population. But a similar analysis of 2004 imprisonment data by sentencing scholar Michael Tonry found that only 61% of the black incarceration rate is explained by disproportionate engagement in criminal behavior. Thus, nearly 40% of the racial disparity in incarceration today cannot be explained by differential offending patterns.

A 1994 state-based assessment of these issues found broad variation in the extent to which higher crime rates among African Americans explained disproportionate imprisonment (Robert D. Crutchfield, George S. Bridges & Susan R. Pitchford: *Analytical and Aggregation Biases in Analyses of*

Imprisonment: Reconciling Discrepancies in Studies of Racial Disparity, J. Res. Crime & Delinq. 166, 179 1994).

Thus, while greater involvement in some crimes is related to higher rates of incarceration for African Americans, the weight of the evidence to date suggests that a significant proportion of the disparities is not a function of disproportionate criminal behavior.

> ## Disparities in Criminal Justice Processing

Despite changes in leadership and growing attention to issues of racial and ethnic disparity in recent years, these disparities in criminal justice decision making still persist at every level of the criminal justice system. This does not necessarily suggest that these outcomes represent conscious efforts to discriminate but they nonetheless contribute to excessive rates of imprisonment for some groups.

Disparities in processing have been seen most prominently in the area of law enforcement, with documentation of widespread racial profiling in recent years. National surveys conducted by the U.S. Department of Justice find that while African Americans may be subject to traffic stops by police at similar rates to whites, and they are three times as likely to be searched after being stopped.

Disparate practices of law enforcement related to the *war on drugs* have been well documented in many jurisdictions and in combination with sentencing policies, represent the most significant contributor to disproportionate rates of incarceration. This effect has come about through two overlapping trends. First, the escalation of the drug war has produced a remarkable rise in the number of people in prisons and jails either awaiting trial or serving time for a drug offense –

increasing from 40,000 in 1980 to 500,000 today. Second, a general law enforcement emphasis on drug-related policing in communities of color has resulted in African Americans being prosecuted for drug offenses far out of proportion to the degree that they use or sell drugs.

In 2005, African Americans represented 14% of current drug users, yet they constituted 33.9% of persons arrested for a drug offense and 53% of persons sentenced to prison for a drug offense. Evidence of racial profiling by law enforcement does not suggest by any means that all agencies or all officers engage in such behaviors. In fact, in recent years, many police agencies have initiated training and oversight measures designed to prevent and identify such practices. Nevertheless, such behaviors still persist and clearly thwart efforts to promote racial justice.

> ## Overlap of Race and Class Effects

Disparities in the criminal justice system are in part a function of the interrelationship between race and class and reflect the disadvantages faced by low income defendants. This can be seen most prominently in regard to the quality of defense counsel. While many public defenders and appointed counsel provide high quality legal support, in far too many jurisdictions the defense bar is characterized by high caseloads, poor training, and inadequate resources.

In an assessment of this situation, the American Bar Association concluded that, "too often the lawyers who provide defense services are inexperienced, fail to maintain adequate client contact, and furnish services that are simply not competent." The limited availability of private resources disadvantages low-income people in other ways as well. For example, in considering whether a defendant will be released from jail prior to trial, owning a telephone is one factor used in making a recommendation so that the court can stay in contact with the defendant.

But for persons who do not own a phone this seemingly innocuous requirement becomes an obstacle to pretrial release.

At the sentencing stage, low-income substance abusers are also disadvantaged compared to defendants with resources. Given the general shortage of treatment programs, a defendant who has private insurance to cover the cost of treatment is in a much better position to make an argument for a non-incarcerative sentence than one who depends on publicly funded treatment programs.

➤ Impact of Race Neutral Policies

Sentencing and related criminal justice policies that are ostensibly *race neutral* have in fact been seen over many years to have clear racial effects that could have been anticipated by legislators prior to enactment. Research on the development of punitive sentencing policies sheds light on the relationship between harsh sanctions and public perceptions of race. Criminologist Ted Chiricos and colleagues found that among whites, support for harsh sentencing policies was correlated with the degree to which a particular crime was perceived to be a "black" crime. (Ted Chiricos, Kelly Welch & Marc Gertz, *Racial Typification of Crime and Support for Punitive Measures*, 42 Criminology 359, 374, 2004).)

The federal crack cocaine sentencing laws of the 1980s received significant attention due to their highly disproportionate racial outcomes but other policies have produced similar effects. For example, a number of states and the federal government have adopted "school zone" drug laws that penalize drug offenses that take place within a certain distance of a school more harshly than other drug crimes. *The racial effect of these laws is an outgrowth of housing patterns. Because urban areas are more densely populated than suburban or rural areas, city residents are much more likely to be within a short distance of a school than are residents of suburban or rural areas.*

And because African Americans are more likely to live in urban neighborhoods than are whites, African Americans convicted of a drug offense are subject to harsher penalties than whites committing a similar offense in a less-populated area. A state commission analysis of a school zone drug law in New Jersey, for example, documented that 96% of the persons serving prison time for such offenses were African American or Latino.

Such broad statistics mask the racial disparity that pervades the U.S. criminal justice system, and for African Americans in particular. African Americans are more likely than white Americans to be arrested.

Once arrested, they are more likely to be convicted and once convicted they are more likely to experience lengthy prison sentences. African American adults are 6.0 times more likely to be incarcerated than whites and Hispanics are three times as likely. As of 2001, 1 in 3 black boys born in that year could expect to go to prison in his lifetime, as could 1 of every 6 Latinos compared to 1 in 17 white boys. Racial and ethnic disparities among women are less substantial than among men but remain prevalent.

The source of such disparities is deeper and more systemic than explicit racial discrimination. The United States in effect operates two distinct criminal justice systems: one for wealthy people and another for poor people and people of color. The wealthy can access a vigorous adversary system replete with constitutional protections for defendants. Yet the experiences of poor and minority defendants within the criminal justice system often differ substantially from that model due to a number of factors, each of which contributes to the overrepresentation of such individuals in the system. As former Georgetown Law Professor David Cole states in his book *No Equal Justice;* "These double standards are not of course, explicit. On the face of it, the criminal law is color-blind and class blind. But in a sense, this only makes the problem worse. The rhetoric of the criminal justice system sends the message that our society carefully protects everyone's constitutional rights, but in practice the rules assure that law enforcement prerogatives will generally prevail over the rights of minorities and the poor. By affording criminal suspects substantial constitutional rights in theory, the Supreme Court validates the results of the criminal justice system as fair. That formal fairness obscures the systemic concerns that ought to be raised by the fact that the prison population is overwhelmingly poor and disproportionately black."

By creating and perpetuating policies that allow such racial disparities to exist in its criminal justice system, the United States is in violation of its obligations under Article 2 and Article 26 of the International Covenant on Civil and Political Rights to ensure that all its residents – regardless of race are treated equally under the law. The Sentencing Project notes that the United Nations Special Rapporteur is working to consult with U.S. civil society organizations on contemporary forms of racism, racial discrimination, and related intolerance. Established in 1986, the Sentencing Project works for a fair and effective U.S. criminal justice system by promoting reforms in sentencing policy, addressing unjust racial disparities and practices, and advocating for alternatives to incarceration. The staff of The Sentencing Project have testified before the U.S. Congress and state legislative bodies and have submitted briefs to the Supreme Court of the United States on various issues related to incarceration and criminal justice policy. The organization's research findings are regularly relied upon by policymakers and covered by major news outlets.

Racial Disparity in the United States Criminal Justice System

A. Policing

In 2016, black Americans comprised 27% of all individuals arrested in the United States – double their share of the total population.

Black youth accounted for 15% of all U.S. children yet made up 35% of juvenile arrests in that year. What might appear at first to be a linkage between race and crime is in large part a function of concentrated urban poverty, which is far more common for African Americans than for other racial groups. This accounts for a substantial portion of African Americans' increased likelihood of committing certain violent and property crimes.

But while there is a higher African American rate of involvement in certain crimes, white Americans overestimate the proportion of crime committed by African Americans and Latinos, overlook the fact that communities of color are disproportionately victims of crime and discount the prevalence of bias in the criminal justice system.

In 1968, the Kerner Commission called on the country to make, "massive and sustained investments in jobs and education to reverse the segregation and poverty that have created in the racial ghetto a destructive environment totally unknown to most white Americans." Fifty years later, the commission's lone surviving member concluded that, "In many ways, things have gotten no better or have gotten worse." The rise of mass incarceration begins with disproportionate levels of police contact with African Americans. This is striking in particular for drug offenses, which are committed at roughly equal rates across races. "One reason minorities are stopped disproportionately is because police see violations where they are," said Louis Dekmar, the president of the International Association of Chiefs of Police and chief of LaGrange, Georgia's police department. The chief added: "Crime is often significantly higher in minority neighborhoods than elsewhere. And that is where we allocate our resources." Dekmar's view is not uncommon. Absent meaningful efforts to address societal segregation and disproportionate levels of poverty, U.S. criminal justice policies have cast a dragnet targeting African Americans. The War on Drugs as well as policing policies including *Broken Windows* and *Stop, Question, and Frisk*. This includes higher levels of police contact with innocent people and higher levels of arrests for drug crimes. Thus, 1 in 4 people arrested for drug law violations in 2015 was African American, although drug use rates do not differ substantially by race and ethnicity and drug users generally purchase drugs from people of the same race or ethnicity. For example, the ACLU found that African Americans were four times more likely to be arrested for marijuana possession than whites in 2010, even though their rate of marijuana usage was comparable.

The highest officials in New York City had, "Turned a blind eye to the evidence that officers are conducting stops in a racially discriminatory manner," Judge Shira A. Scheindlin concluded regarding the city's stop and frisk tactic, declaring it unconstitutional in 2013. The policy, which broadly targeted male residents of neighborhoods populated by low-income people of color to uncover drugs and weapons, was shown to be ineffective and this assessment was further validated when New York City continued its crime decline after scaling back stop and frisk. Yet other localities continue to deploy the practice.

New York City, like many other cities, remains reluctant to scale back *Broken Windows Policing*, a public safety approach that relies on clamping down on petty offenses and neighborhood disorder. Between 2001 and 2013, 51% of the city's population over age 16 was African American or Hispanic.

Yet during that period, 82% of those arrested for misdemeanors were African American or Hispanic as were 81% of those who received summonses for violations of the administrative code (including such behaviors as public consumption of alcohol, disorderly conduct, and bicycling on the sidewalk). Yet research showed that order maintenance strategies have had only a modest impact on serious crime rates and have caused great damage to communities of color.

These strategies also expose people of color to a greater risk of being killed during a police encounter. In addition to pursuing policies that bring little gain in crime reduction and impose great costs on people of color, policymakers and criminal justice leaders have been late to address discriminatory policies for which they provide no justification such as biased use of officer discretion and revenue driven policing. In recent years, black drivers have been somewhat more likely to be stopped than whites but have been far more likely to be searched and arrested. The causes and outcomes of these stops differ by race, and staggering racial disparities in rates of police stops persist in certain jurisdictions pointing to unchecked racial bias, whether intentional or not and at the officers discretion. A closer look at the causes of traffic stops reveals that police are more likely to stop African American and Hispanic drivers for discretionary reasons such as *investigatory stops* (proactive stops used to investigate drivers deemed suspicious) rather than *traffic-safety stops* (reactive stops used to enforce traffic laws or vehicle codes).

Nationwide surveys also reveal disparities in the outcomes of police stops. Once pulled over, African American and Hispanic drivers were three times as likely as whites to be searched (6% and 7% versus 2%) and black people were twice as likely as white drivers to be arrested. These patterns hold even though police officers generally have a *lower contraband hit rate* when they search black versus white drivers. Ferguson's law enforcement practices are shaped by the city's focus on revenue rather than by public safety needs, the Civil Rights Division of the Department of Justice (DOJ) concluded in 2015 after the police killing of Michael Brown brought national attention to police community tensions in the St. Louis, Missouri suburb. The DOJ found that black residents' disproportionate rate of police stops, searches, and arrests resulted from city officials' growing reliance on municipal fines and fees which police officers and court officers were exhorted to deliver through aggressive enforcement of traffic violations and petty offenses. Arch City Defenders; authors of an early and influential paper on the troubled municipal court system demonstrated that many other St. Louis municipalities have similar or worse practices than Ferguson.

B. Pretrial

African Americans were incarcerated in local jails at a rate four times that of non-Hispanic whites in 2016. These disparities stem in part from the policies and practices of policing described earlier but are compounded by those introduced at this stage of processing. Given that nearly two-thirds (65%) of people in jail in 2016 were being detained prior to trial, policies and decisions influencing pretrial detention play a key role in driving the disparity in the jail population and beyond.

Pretrial detention has been shown to increase the odds of conviction and people who are detained awaiting trial are also more likely to accept less favorable plea deals, to be sentenced to prison, and to receive longer sentences. Seventy percent of pretrial releases require money bond, an especially high hurdle for low-income defendants who are disproportionately people of color.

African Americans and Latinos are more likely than whites to be denied bail, have a higher money bond set and to be detained because they cannot pay their bond. They are often assessed to be higher safety and flight risks because they are more likely to experience socioeconomic disadvantage and to have criminal records. Implicit bias also contributes to people of color faring worse than comparable whites in bail determinations.

C. Sentencing

Although African Americans and Latinos comprise 29% of the U.S. population, they make up 57% of the U.S. prison population. This results in imprisonment rates for African American and Hispanic adults that are 5.9 and 3.1 times the rate for white adults, respectively and at far higher levels in some states. Notably, these disparities exist for both the least and most serious offenses. Of the 277,000 people imprisoned nationwide for a drug offense, over half (56%) are African American or Latino. Nearly half (48%) of the

206,000 people serving life and virtual life prison sentences are African American and another 15% are Latino. Among youth, African Americans are 4.1 times as likely to be committed to secure placements as whites, Native American are 3.1 times as likely and Hispanics are 1.5 times as likely. Although levels of youth confinement have significantly declined in recent years the racial gap between African American and Native Americans versus white youth has increased.

The racial disparities in the adult and juvenile justice systems stem in part from policing and pretrial factors that are compounded by discretionary decisions and sentencing policies that disadvantage people of color because of their race or higher rates of socioeconomic disadvantage. Prosecutors are more likely to charge people of color with crimes that carry heavier sentences than whites. Federal prosecutors, for example, are twice as likely to charge African Americans with offenses that carry a mandatory minimum sentence than similarly situated whites. State prosecutors are also more likely to charge African American rather than similar white defendants under habitual offender laws.

Policies that disadvantage people of color face such as drug free school zone laws mandate sentencing enhancements for people caught selling drugs in designated school zones. The expansive geographic range of these zones coupled with high urban density has disproportionately affected residents of urban areas, and particularly those in high-poverty areas who are largely people of color. Legislators in New Jersey scaled back their state law after a study found that 96% of persons subject to these enhancements were African American or Latino. All 50 states and the District of Columbia have some form of drug-free school zone law. Most jurisdictions inadequately fund their indigent defense programs.

While there are many high quality public defender offices, in far too many cases indigent individuals are represented by public defenders with excessively high caseloads, or by assigned counsel with limited experience in criminal defense. Public defenders in Louisiana for example, had sued the state and those in Kansas City, Missouri protested their crushing caseloads.

D. Parole

During the era of mass incarceration, a declining proportion of the prison population has a sentence that allows for discretionary release on parole, as lawmakers have required courts to shift from indeterminate sentences (whose release requires a discretionary parole decision) to fixed-term sentences (which have set release dates). Among sentences that allow for discretionary parole release, the process can be harder for people of color.

Some research suggests that parole boards are influenced by an applicant's race in their decision making, though more research is needed in this area. Racial bias among correctional officers also shapes parole outcomes. As revealed by a New York Times investigation on New York prisons, comparable in-prison conduct; a major determinant of parole decisions which may result in divergent prison disciplinary records for blacks and Latinos versus whites.

Based on an analysis of almost 60,000 disciplinary cases from the state's prisons, reporters found that disparities in discipline were greatest for infractions that gave discretion to guards, such as disobeying a direct order. Underinvestment and racial disparities also persist in community supervision with many parole and probation systems offering supervision with little support, and with evidence that parole and probation officers are more likely to revoke people of color than whites for comparable behavior. For example, the Urban Institute's examination of probation revocation rates in Dallas County, Texas, Iowa's Sixth Judicial District, Multnomah County, Oregon, and New York City revealed that black probationers were revoked at disproportionate rates in all study sites at levels which raise concerns about the presence of bias to the disadvantage of black probationers.

E. Post Prison/Collateral Consequences

African Americans are most exposed to the collateral consequences associated with a criminal record. In 2010, 8% of all adults in the United States had a felony conviction on their record. Among African American men, the rate was 1 in 3 (33%). People with criminal records face a host of obstacles to re-enter society even after they have fully completed their term of incarceration or community supervision. These include barriers to securing steady employment and housing to accessing the social safety net and federal student aid to exercising the right to vote. Nearly one-third of U.S. workers hold jobs that require an occupational license, a requirement which sometimes bars and often poses cumbersome obstacles for people with criminal records.

In sectors that do not require licensing, employers are 50% less likely to call back white job applicants with incarceration histories than comparable applicants without prison records. African American job applicants who are less likely to receive call backs than whites to begin with experience an even more pronounced discrimination related to a criminal record.

White people with criminal records receive more favorable treatment than black people and people of color without criminal records.

People with criminal convictions also face discrimination in the private rental market and those with felony drug convictions face restrictions in accessing government assisted housing. The Welfare Reform Act of 1996 imposed a lifetime denial of cash assistance and food stamps to people convicted in state or federal courts of felony drug offenses, unless states opt out of the ban. Given the dynamics of social class and the accompanying disparate racial effects of the criminal justice system, women and children of color are disproportionately impacted by this exclusionary law. By 2018, twenty four states had fully opted out of the food stamp ban, twenty-one other states had only done so in part and five states continued to fully enforce the ban.

An even larger number of states continue to impose a partial or full ban on cash assistance for people with felony drug convictions. Disenfranchisement patterns have also reflected the dramatic growth and disproportionate impact of criminal convictions. A record 6.1 million Americans were forbidden from voting because of their felony record in 2016, rising from 1.2 million in 1976. Felony disenfranchisement rates for voting age for African Americans reached 7.4% in 2016 – four times the rate of non-African Americans (1.8%). In three states, more than 1 in 5 voting-age African Americans were disenfranchised: Florida, Kentucky, and Tennessee. The majority of disenfranchised Americans are living in their communities having fully completed their sentences or remaining supervised while on probation or parole.

In 2018, The House passed a Farm Bill that would force at least two million people off of vital nutrition assistance by making harmful changes to the Supplemental Nutrition Assistance Program (SNAP). SNAP is a vital resource for many leaving prisons and jails and returning to communities. Programs like SNAP that help individuals and families meet their basic living standards are particularly useful for weathering the societal barriers and stigma of a criminal record. SNAP should be made even stronger, not weaker for formerly incarcerated. Every year, 626,000 people return to communities from the prison system. Federal, state, and local policies block formerly incarcerated people from rejoining neighborhoods, workplaces, and schools. In some instances, drug convictions bar students from grants, loans, and work study through the Higher Education Act of 1988. To varying degrees, states also implement automatic driver's license suspension for anyone convicted of a drug offense. Even without specific policies against formerly incarcerated people, discrimination based on a criminal record is legal and common. Local public housing providers, for example, use their discretion to temporarily or permanently ban formerly incarcerated people from affordable housing.

Congress' Farm Bill is a misguided policy to cut SNAP access under the guise of *work requirements* and is an especially bad idea for returning citizens. This proposal would cut off SNAP benefits to individuals, including parents, if they are not able to find work or enter a qualified job training program within just a month. Employment-based exclusion from SNAP builds on the job discrimination that returning citizens already face. Except where prohibited by state or local law, private and government employers can disqualify formerly incarcerated people from job interviews with a single application question about criminal history.

Job-seekers returning from prison face more than a job search – they have to (re)connect with friends and family, (re)enroll in Medicaid, find an apartment, and more. For those who find willing employers while on probation, officer meetings and drug testing can be hurdles to scheduling job interviews and work hours. Therefore, formerly incarcerated people are more likely to need SNAP and less likely to find steady employment, regardless of workforce development programs as Congress' Farm Bill claims to offer.

These challenges to reentry make SNAP an even more critical resource. The Supplemental Nutrition Assistance Program, or SNAP, serves over 40 million people. About two thirds of this group are children, elderly, or have disabilities. Beyond lifting 10% of its households above the poverty line, SNAP keeps working families secure and stable. Costs of incarceration like court debts, high prison phone rates, and visitation travel also make nearly 50% of families with incarcerated members struggle to meet basic food and housing need

Even without the additional barriers to accessing SNAP included in the Farm Bill, SNAP has specific prohibitions for many individuals with a criminal record. Current federal law permanently disqualifies individuals with drug felony convictions from SNAP. In 1996, a push for "welfare reform" created the drug felony ban on SNAP and TANF, or Temporary Assistance for Needy Families. While this ban does not apply to all 100 million Americans with a criminal record, it sets a harmful moral standard for punishment above and beyond prison sentences. The justice system should not jeopardize a person's right to eat. Limiting SNAP threatens the health of returning citizens and their families. Under the ban, formerly incarcerated parents are only allowed benefits on behalf of their children, which strains family budgets.

There is some good news at the state level. On the SNAP ban and other policies, states are leading the way to reduce collateral consequences. Only four states have left the federal SNAP and TANF bans in place as written – the rest have realized they needed to change. Some states have removed the SNAP and TANF bans altogether, and most states have limited the ban by making it only apply to certain offenses, time limits, or exempting drug treatment program participants.

In 2017, four state legislatures – Indiana, Louisiana, North Dakota, and Maryland increased access to SNAP for formerly incarcerated people. 31 states and 150 cities, covering 75% of the country's population have prohibited asking for criminal history in initial job applications and required background checks to come later in the application process.

Instead of putting SNAP even further out of reach for formerly incarcerated people with program restrictions, Congress should increase access to reentry programs, basic needs, and employment. SNAP at its core provides the food security we all need to survive and thrive. No criminal punishment or record should keep food off of the table.

The Second Chance Reauthorization Act (H.R. 2899) would fund local reentry programs to support returning citizens from prisons and jails.

The **Second Chance Reauthorization Act of 2015** would:

- Reauthorize the most successful Second Chance programs, including reentry demonstration grants and mentoring grants, grants for family-based substance use treatment and other SUD services, and grants for education and career preparation

- Expand opportunities for community-based nonprofits to apply for grant programs for which they are currently ineligible to receive direct funding

- Specifically identifies medication-assisted treatment as a supported activity for reentry courts funded by the reentry demonstration grants program

- Require coordination among multiple federal agencies, state and local government, and service providers on federal programs and policies related to reentry

- Modify the Second Chance careers training grant program to support programs that provide job training for a wider range of occupations

- Expand the mentoring grants program to support employment services, substance use and mental health treatment, housing, and other transitional services

The **REDEEM Act** (H.R. 1209, S. 827) would help people with nonviolent offenses seal or expunge their records, making them eligible to register for SNAP and apply to jobs without prior convictions to list.

Providing formerly incarcerated individuals with the tools to effectively reintegrate into society is essential in preventing recidivism. One in three American adults currently has a criminal record. Unfortunately, over two-thirds of formerly-incarcerated people are rearrested within three years. Removing collateral consequences, including barriers to employment, education, and benefits, is one way to address this troubling trend.

"Tragically, in today's world, a criminal record has become a life sentence carrying with it the possibility – and all too often, the reality – of it negatively affecting one's employment, housing, access to credit, child support, and so many other issues. We know that sentences issued by our criminal justice system disproportionately affect Americans of color," said Chairman Cummings. "The bill we introduced today will seal and expunge offenses committed by a child, provide a path for adults to seal their non-violent criminal records to ease re-entry, and help ensure that a criminal record does not become a life sentence.

Future generations are counting on us to reform our broken criminal justice system now so they can see a system and an entire country in which they can believe."

Specifically, the **REDEEM Act**:

- Incentivizes states to increase the age of criminal responsibility to 18 years old: Currently, several states have set the original jurisdiction age of adult criminal courts below 18 years old. This sends countless kids into the unforgiving adult criminal justice system. The REDEEM Act incentivizes states to change that by offering preference to Community Oriented Policing Services (COPS) grant applicants to those that have set 18 or older as the age of original jurisdiction for adult criminal courts.

- Allows for sealing and expungement of juvenile records: The bill would provide for the automatic expungement of records for juveniles who committed non-violent crimes before they turned 15 years old and the automatic sealing of records for juveniles who committed non-violent crimes.

- Restricts use of juvenile solitary confinement: The bill would end the cruel and counterproductive practice of solitary confinement except in the most extreme circumstances in which it is necessary to protect a juvenile detainee or those around them. When confinement is necessary, the bill places strict time and condition limitations.

- Offers adults a way to seal non-violent criminal records: The bill provides the first broad-based federal path to the sealing of criminal records for adults. The bill would provide for the automatic sealing of records of non-violent drug offenses. In addition, those who commit other non-violent offenses will be able to petition a court and make their case for the sealing of records. Furthermore, employers requesting FBI background checks will only receive relevant and accurate information – thereby protecting job applicants – because of bill provisions to improve the background check system.

- Lifts ban on SNAP and TANF benefits for low-level drug offenders: The bill restores access to benefits for those who have served their time for use, possession, and distribution crimes.

The REDEEM Act has been endorsed by the Center for Law and Social Policy, the National Employment Law Project, Just Leadership USA, Campaign for Youth Justice, The Sentencing Project, the Leadership Conference on Civil and Human Rights, National Crittenton, and the Interfaith Action for Human Rights.

IV.

Broken Promises: Failure of Law Enforcement in the Black Community

The nationwide unrest that follows Floyd's death is undoubtedly more intense than in 2014; the leadership from the White House immeasurably more reckless, insensitive and life threatening.

And yet, here the country is again in 2020.

Violence against black men and women and children and other people of color at the hands of white authority is foundational to the United States, and continues to influence its policing culture to this day.

Precursors to modern-day American police departments include violent slave patrols utilized in southern states before the civil war, then the legal enforcement of racist Black Codes, followed by Jim Crow laws. Early municipal departments in growing US cities were overwhelmingly white, and brutalized vulnerable communities routinely. Thousands of lynchings of black Americans by white vigilantes went unpunished by the judicial system. And during the civil rights era and well beyond, peaceful protest has been harshly suppressed by officers sworn to protect and serve.

Trump presented himself as the "law and order" candidate during a dark acceptance speech. The former Milwaukee sheriff David Clarke led the arena in a chilling round of applause for the Baltimore police officer Brian Rice, who that day had been acquitted on charges related to the death of Freddie Gray, whose spine was almost severed during his 2014 arrest. Trump thrust the issue of race and policing firmly into the culture wars he was fomenting. Trump's response to police violence was a marked departure from the Obama administrations. Since Michael Brown's death, which began a nationwide reckoning and rejuvenated the Black Lives Matter movement, Obama had used his authority to target problematic police departments, including those in Ferguson, Chicago and Baltimore, with justice department investigations. He issued an executive order to curtail local departments' procurement of certain military-grade equipment. He commissioned a taskforce on 21st-century policing, which memorably urged American law enforcement to move from a "warrior" to a "guardian" culture.

Although America has a sprawling, decentralized system of policing – the country has roughly 18,000 police departments each with their own use of force policy, hiring practices and oversight mechanisms making universal reform near impossible – there were at least signs of tentative progress.

And then Donald Trump became the 45th president of the United States.

For decades, Americans have talked constantly about a "no-snitch black" culture hampering police investigations leaving violent criminals on the streets. But what about the no-snitch police culture that has hampered investigations into officer misconduct, leaving violent criminal police officers on the streets?

Police officers should lead the way in fostering an American civic culture of reporting lawbreakers. It is *their* professional duty to snitch to enforce the law first and foremost against themselves. How can they expect citizens to *snitch* to them if they refuse to? How can they expect citizens to trust the criminal justice system if the police don't trust the criminal justice system? Snitching on each other remains their only salvation from this hypocrisy; their best tool for building trust with the communities they purport to serve and protect. But first, they'll have to grapple with an empirical truth: communities of color are actually disproportionately likely to report crimes – it's police themselves who have maintained a culture of silence.

That's not something most law enforcement leaders seem inclined to acknowledge. "Law enforcement as a whole has been unfairly maligned and blamed for the unacceptable deeds of a few bad actors," complained Attorney General Jeff Sessions in February 2017. "There is no Blue Wall of Silence. No cops are covering for cops." "It's not that we're all out here covering for one another," said Sergeant Dan Hils, president of the Cincinnati Police Union. "Loyalty ends with criminal activity."

Since the 1980s, police officers have grumbled of a growing no-snitch culture – not within their own ranks but outside their blue wall in African American and Latino neighborhoods. "I have been in hospital rooms, or in the street standing over somebody being loaded into an ambulance, and they refuse to talk and you think, "What in the world are we here for?" Sergeant Mike Huff said in Tulsa. The mix of neighborhood anecdotes, police reports, media stories, no-snitch videos, apparel and television shows, and music lyrics have baked the popular belief in a no-snitch black culture, even among black people. The "no-snitch mentality is killing the black community," a black prisoner serving a life sentence proclaimed in the Toledo Blade in 2014. Police defenders like to point to the falling clearance rate for homicides as proof not of the falling clearance rate, but of the no-snitch black culture. In 1965, the rate of homicide cases ending in an arrest was more than ninety percent. By 2015, the rate had fallen to 64.1%

Anecdotal evidence persists about individuals of all races refusing to report crimes. But evidence of uniquely black cultural hostility to snitching does not exist – it is yet another racist idea without any evidentiary standing. But when did Americans ever need evidence to believe something was culturally or behaviorally wrong with black people as a group? Racist ideas are believable, not provable. The evidence points to black communities perhaps being more likely to snitch than white communities and Latino communities being the most likely to snitch.

The National Crime Victimization Survey compiled each year by the Bureau of Justice Statistics found in 2010 that violence against black people and white people were reported at nearly identical rates while violence against Latinos was the most likely to be reported. The latest National Crime Victimization Survey in 2016 again found violence against Latinos (52%) was more likely to be reported to the police than violence against African American and whites (40%). For serious violent crimes, violence against Latinos (65%) and African Americans (60%) was far more likely to be reported to the police than violence against Caucasians (45%). But these statistics did not inflame the policing community to start lamenting about a no-snitch white culture.

Black youth are especially branded with a no-snitch culture, without evidence, and in the face of evidence to the contrary. Preliminary data from a survey administered to 1,500 community college students showed that if the perpetrator was a relative or a friend, whites were less likely to snitch than non-whites, despite whites reporting they trust the police far more than African Americans and despite twice as many African Americans reporting they listened to music that ridiculed snitching. Urban, black high school dropouts may be the most maligned for not reporting crimes to police officers. And yet, police officers ironically, rely on snitching especially from the hyper-incarcerated population of black high school dropouts. The staggering volume of arrests of African American and Latino youth over the last four decades would have ground the criminal-justice system to a halt if every single case went to trial. Plea agreements – defendants snitching on themselves and often snitching on others in exchange for more lenient sentences have become as endemic as police informants in African American and Latino neighborhoods. 9 out of 10 federal cases, for example, end in plea agreements.

Police officers however, do not appear to be commonly snitching on themselves, and accepting plea agreements. There is a no-snitch police culture that may be as widespread and harmful as the myth of a no-snitch black culture. The National Institute of Ethics surveyed 3,714 officers and academic recruits from 42 states in 1999 and 2000. A no-snitching code of silence commonly exists, responded 79% of officers. More than half of the officers said this no-snitch code does not bother them. Nearly half of the officers reported witnessing misconduct and not reporting it. That's probably because 73% of responding officers said they'd be fired if they snitched. And 73% of the officers said the individuals pressuring them to keep quiet were leaders. In

2001, a national survey of police attitudes conducted by the Police Foundation found that a majority of officers said turning a "blind eye" to police misconduct was not unusual. Meanwhile, roughly two-thirds reported that *they did not always report serious criminal violations by fellow officers and because they'd be given the cold shoulder* if they did.

In his forward to that report, the Police Foundation's president, Hubert Williams, wrote, "Most of America's police officers are honest, dedicated, hard-working public servants, and it is they, as well as the public they serve who are victims of bad cops." If most police officers are good, then they are being forced to operate in a bad policing culture where the personal desire to report misconduct is tempered by the top down forces to remain silent or, by their own self-interest of keeping their jobs and staying out of prison.

Even when undercover Atlanta officers fired 39 shots at 92-year-old Kathryn Johnston in 2006 after busting into the wrong home, they refused to snitch. They planted drugs to cover themselves. Caught in their lies, two officers finally pled guilty and received reduced sentences. Three officers were imprisoned. Two years ago, when San Francisco officers accused a sergeant of making racist and sexist comments, the former head and acting consultant of the city's police union called them "snitches."

And then there's the tragic death of 17-year-old LaQuan McDonald in 2014. Chicago police officer Jason Van Dyke claimed he opened fire after the teenager lunged at him with a knife, a claim backed up by on the scene reports from three other officers.

The dashcam video contradicted their claims, sparking protests that compelled former Chicago mayor Rahm Emanuel to acknowledge the "blue wall of silence" in 2015. The

Justice Department's investigations of the Chicago and Baltimore police departments discovered broken systems of silence. *When officers have stepped forward in Baltimore the report found, fellow officers have retaliated against them.*

In 2011, when a Baltimore detective asked a sergeant about reporting two fellow officers who brutally beat a suspect he said the sergeant replied: "If you are a rat, your career is done." The good cop decided to be a rat. And the good cop's career in Baltimore was done. The day before Baltimore detective Sean Suiter was scheduled to testify in a grand-jury hearing against fellow officers, he died from a shot by his own handgun. His death remains unsolved – one of the only unsolved deaths of a police officer in Baltimore's history. When will police departments focus more on rooting out their own no-snitching culture that undermines their job duties than on attacking a no-snitch black culture that does not exist? Not snitching is not a black problem, a white problem, a poor problem, an urban problem or a youth problem. Not snitching is an American problem that extends to all ethnicities. When will police officers model for Americans the difficult civic duty of snitching against partners, against close friends, against violent neighbors? When will they show us by their actions that legality must trump loyalty, career and fear?

Police officers MUST be comfortable snitching and the public need to be comfortable snitching to them. Too often the response to the report of a minor crime like breaking car windows or no crime at all has ended in a life being lost and an officer back on duty weeks later. Part of us want to keep police guns as far away from black bodies as we can because we fear their guns and they fear our bodies. Why would African American play Russian roulette by reporting a crime? It would be much easier for them to report crimes if they trusted police officers around black bodies. If black lives mattered more than police fear, if arrests actually reduced crime and if resources were going to rehabilitate human beings rather than cage them like they are animals, imagine what a remarkable society it would be to reside in.

Black people in other words have every reason not to report crimes. And yet, the evidence shows we still do – even as we are ridiculed for doing so. Police officers on the other hand have every reason to snitch and yet they commonly do not – and get praised for doing so.

Meanwhile, statistics show police are arguably failing to pro-tect residents in black communities. While black people made up about 13% of the population in 2015, they made up more than half of reported murder victims. 2016 Pew Research Center survey found that black people are less than half as likely to trust the police as their white counterparts. When asked whether police treat racial and ethnic groups equally, 75% of white people said cops do an excellent or good job in this area, while just 35% of black people said the same. And 75% of white people said police do a good or excellent job using the right amount of force for each situation, while just 33% of black people did. Thomas Abt, a criminologist at Harvard University, put it in stark terms: "In addition to all of these burdens that we're placing on African-American communities in terms of aggressive policing, we're funda-mentally failing them at keeping them safe."

Policing in America can be fixed. Over the years, I've spoken to different law enforcement agencies, politicians and policy makers about how to address complaints of racial bias while making sure communities are effectively policed for crime. Here are some examples:

➢ **Defund, Dismantle and Rebuild the American police force**

Defunding the police force is a good start but overall, it doesn't affect police departments throughout America. After 168 years of structural racism, police departments are woefully infected with corruption, cowardice, racism and bigotry. **NOTE:** I'm not asking to dismantle the police force. What I want to see however, is the ***dismantling of structural racist policies*** that for more than 100 years have allowed police to violate the human rights of African Americans and other people of color.

➢ **Demilitarized the police**

More than 8,000 local police forces, including more than 100 college police agencies, have received over $5 billion in military equipment from the federal government under the "1033 Program." The militarization of policing has become commonplace in towns across America. Local police routinely have automatic weapons and heavily armored military vehicles. They have camouflage combat fatigues, flash-bang grenades and night-vision rifle scopes.

➢ **End Qualified Immunity**

This is a judicially created doctrine that shields government officials from being held personally liable for constitutional violations – like the right to be free from excessive police force. More corrupt police officers hide behind this doctrine than honest cops.

➤ Police need to apologize for centuries of abuse

Time and time again, we hear the same thing from multiple experts: Until police own up to how minority communities view them, they won't be able to effectively police their communities. Some police officers might feel many of the criticisms are unfair. Some might hear about the history of police being used on slave patrols and feel that they are wrongly blamed for things they weren't even alive for. Some might feel that they are good cops and it's only a few officers who are bad. But that doesn't matter. The reality is minority communities distrust police!

That sentiment is based on a long history of flat-out racist policing in America even if it doesn't apply to every single officer or department today. Until police acknowledge that, they will be perceived by many people as trying to cover up a long history of oppression.

David Kennedy, a criminologist at John Jay College argued that there will always be distrust between police and black communities until cops own up to historical abuse. What could a police chief say to an African American and Latino communities? He/she could say, *we recognize these facts – whether we were there or not, whether we were around during slavery, Reconstruction, Jim Crow, attacks on the Civil Rights Movement, or whether it's more recent things that we have done that you have found disrespectful like zero-tolerance policing and high levels of stop and frisk. We are accountable.*

So how can police repair this distrust? For one, experts said police need to undertake a big effort through community meetings, going door to door on their daily patrols, and TV appearances to get their communities aligned with how policing should be done.

➢ Cops should be trained to address their racial biases

Out of all the complaints leveled against the police, the biggest one in recent years – echoed by the Black Lives Matter movement is that police are racially biased. Sometimes the cause is explicit racism such as in North Miami Beach, Florida where police officers used mug shots of black people as target practice.

But other times such biases may occur at the implicit level where people's subconscious biases guide their choices even when they're not fully aware of it. Josh Correll, a University of Colorado psychology professor tested police for racial biases through a shooting simulation. His initial findings showed officers generally did a good job of avoiding shooting unarmed targets of all races. But when shooting was warranted, officers pulled the trigger more quickly against black suspects than white ones. This suggests that officers exhibit some racial bias in shooting.

In the real world, this could lead police to shoot black people at disproportionate rates. Real policing situations after all are often much more complicated. Factors such as a real threat to the officer's life and the chance that a bullet will miss and accidentally hit a passerby can make the situation much more confusing to officers. "In the very situation in which officers most need their training," Correll stated. "We have some reason to believe that their training will most likely fail them," said Correll. That's one of the reasons there are racial disparities in police use of force. An analysis of the available FBI data from 2012 by Vox's Dara Lind found black people accounted for 31% of police killing victims, even though they made up just 13% of the US population.

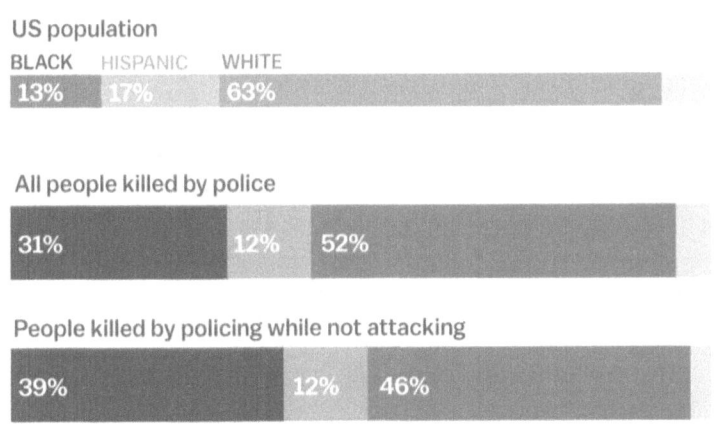

Police kill a disproportionate number of black people

US population

BLACK HISPANIC WHITE

13% 17% 63%

All people killed by police

31% 12% 52%

People killed by policing while not attacking

39% 12% 46%

It's not just individual biases driving the disparities but structural problems as well. As a result of years and years of racial segregation, economic and educational inequality among people of different races, concentrated poverty in minority communities and the criminal justice system's neglect of crimes against minorities, there tends to be much more crime in black neighborhoods. So police are deployed more often in these areas where they're then more likely to shoot and kill someone. But higher crime in minority communities doesn't fully explain the disparities. A 2015 study by researcher Cody Ross found that, "There is no relationship between county level racial bias in police shootings and crime rates. That suggests something else such as potentially racial bias is at work."

Phillip Atiba Goff, a criminal justice and racial bias expert at John Jay College, said, "This isn't about whether officers are all evil racists. Instead, this is a bias that has been found time and time again in just about everyone. If you are a human being chances are you have some level of bias based on race, gender, religion, and so on. But American media and culture with their constant depictions of black people as criminals have shaped Americans' biases into consistently associating black people with criminality."

"The issue of police bias starts with the thing law enforcement is hiring which is that they hire humans," Goff said. "They end up being at least as biased as the rest of the population. And in some instances, I suspect, it may be even slightly more in terms of racial bias." For police, the bias can be particularly bad. They are constantly put in situations where they have to think quickly. And that makes it much more likely that their biases will take over. As Goff said, "If I could put you in the right situation, I could get that particular association to lend itself to certain kinds of behaviors."

Officers can be trained to help combat their biases. Lorie Fridell, a University of South Florida criminologist who works with cops to help them resist their biases previously explained that cops can be taught to force themselves to focus on factors that aren't skin color such as body language and what a person is holding.

Unfortunately, that training is rarely emphasized by police departments. A 2006 report from the Justice Department found that police officers typically receive about 111 hours on firearms skill and self-defense but just 11 hours on cultural diversity and human relations, 8 hours on community policing strategies, and 8 hours on mediation and conflict management.

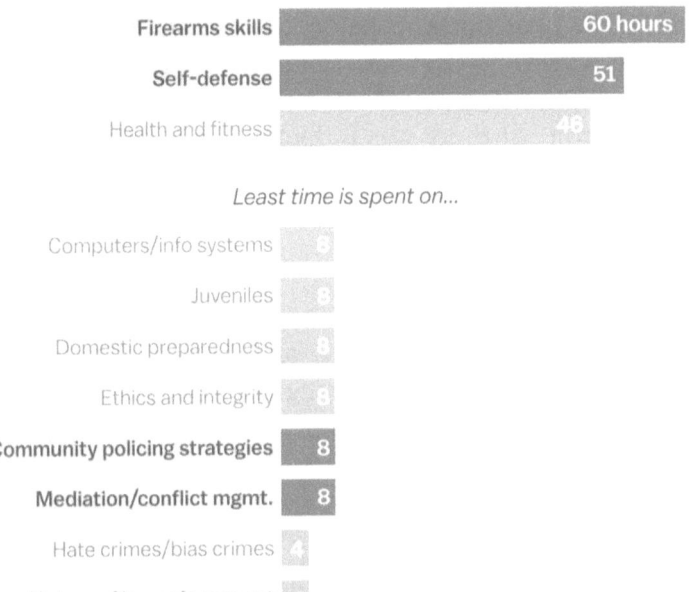

What basic training looks like for state and local police

Most time is spent on...

Firearms skills	60 hours
Self-defense	51
Health and fitness	46

Least time is spent on...

Computers/info systems	8
Juveniles	8
Domestic preparedness	8
Ethics and integrity	8
Community policing strategies	8
Mediation/conflict mgmt.	8
Hate crimes/bias crimes	4
History of law enforcement	4

Data from a 2006 Bureau of Justice Statistics special report
Credit: Alvin Chang

If police want to renew community trust, this needs to change. It likely wouldn't solve all problems however. Racial bias for one, is likely to be present to some degree no matter how well cops are trained. But it would help. Often, the error that leads to an unnecessary shooting and perhaps, bias as a driving factor of excessive force comes long before an officer pulls out his or her gun. It can happen when an officer decides to approach a scene in a certain way.

➢ **Police should avoid situations that lead them to use force**

Think of the final moments before a Cleveland police officer shot and killed 12-year-old Tamir Rice in 2014. In that tragedy, officers suspected that Rice, who was black had an actual firearm, when he was in fact playing with a toy gun. And officers drove right into the park where Rice was playing, shooting the boy within two seconds of getting out of their squad car.

What if officers had instead of driving into the scene parked further away, surveyed the area, and walked into the park more slowly while giving warnings to Rice? It's of course impossible to say what the outcome would be but it certainly seems much more likely that Rice would be alive today.

"We talk about the split-second decisions that have to be made when deadly force is used, and it's a red herring," Goff said. Most of the time, police are not ambushed in a corner and then they have to figure out what to do. Most of the time what happens is there are a number of tactical decisions you've made up until that point that have compromised your safety. So if officers have racial biases and you put them in an intense situation in which according to Goff, they have little to call on but their own biases and those biases are going to guide their actions. "We have to be able to acknowledge and identify the set of situations that are most likely to facilitate biased behavior," Goff said. "And we want to be able to disarm or interrupt them."

Goff gave an example from research work he did in Las Vegas. There, police established a foot pursuit policy that said the officer who was giving chase should not be the first person to put their hands on the suspect. There should be a coordinated backup instead arriving on the scene and taking on that role. The idea is that foot pursuits often ended in excessive use of force because they are high adrenaline chases in which the officer and the suspect can get really angry, really fast. So by limiting when possible, chasing officers from putting their hands on the suspect, Goff figured you could limit use of force.

The change appeared to work. There was a 23% reduction in total use of force and 11% reduction in officer injury over several years, on top of reducing racial disparities, according to Goff. "Safer for the officer, safer for the suspects," he said. "I didn't have to talk about race to reduce a disparity that has racial components to it," he added. "I had to change the fundamental situation where police are chronically engaging with suspects. And that's the kind of example that I'm talking about how you interrupt the biases of life." This is just one example. More broadly, police need to stop being deployed in a way that is particularly aggressive against minority communities such as when cops in New York City effectively targeted people of color and their whole communities through stop and frisk. As Jonathan Blanks, a research associate focused on policing issues at the Cato Institute pointed out, "So long as you have racially disparate policing strategies, you can have all these ideas about how we're going to measure how many black people we stop and reduce bias there. However, I don't think it's really going to work."

➤ **Officers must be held accountable in a very transparent way**

With the above steps, police can avoid more unnecessary uses of force. But there's another problem: when police do use excessive force or engage in other types of misconduct, there needs to be more transparency and accountability in the aftermath. The most well-known policy for this is the adoption of body cameras.

Over the past couple of years, advocates have pushed police departments to equip all their cops with cameras that will record nearly every move.

The cameras are crucial because video can help eliminate some of the doubt for the police and civilians as to what happened for example, a shooting. Take the 2015 police shooting of Walter Scott in North Charleston, South Carolina. An officer, Michael Slager claimed that Scott had tried to take his stun gun and use it on him before fleeing. Video footage from a civilian at the scene however, revealed that Scott had not tried to grab Slager's stun gun, and Slager had shot at Scott's back as the 50-year-old black man very slowly attempted to flee. And after the shooting, Slager then planted the stun gun near Scott's dead body presumably to give his story credibility. If the cell phone video from the passerby didn't exist, would Slager have been charged with murder and civil rights violations? Would he have been fired? Would he have gotten away with a totally unjustified shooting? After all, without video, witness testimony may have been limited to Slager's own account.

Beyond changing the gear that officers wear, some experts argued that police leaders need to embrace a fundamental shift in accountability and transparency. As it stands, police departments are mired in secrecy making it nearly impossible in some cases to find out if an officer has for example, been disciplined in the past. In a 2015 investigation, Robert Lewis, Noah Veltman, and Xander Landen of the New York public radio station WNYC talked to attorneys and experts in all 50 states and Washington, DC, and reviewed laws and court cases to find out which states restrict police disciplinary records. They found that 23 states and DC make the records confidential while 15 other states limit access to records by only letting the public see examples of severe discipline, such as suspension or termination. The remaining 12 states generally open police disciplinary records to the public.

Much of this secrecy is ingrained in police culture. The 'Blue Wall of Silence' tells cops to stay quiet about other officers' misconduct. This code is enforced both formally and informally. In Baltimore for example, the Justice Department found a black sergeant was told to "stay in your lane" when he tried to flag misconduct within the police forced. In 2014, a Baltimore Police Department lieutenant placed several signs next to the desk of an African American sergeant with a reputation for speaking out about alleged misconduct in the department. Among the signs were warnings to "worry about yourself," "mind your own business!!!" and "don't spread rumors!!!" After the sergeant filed a complaint about the signs, the lieutenant admitted to creating them and placing them next to the sergeant's desk. Yet, BPD took no meaningful corrective action. Though the complaint was sustained, the lieutenant received no suspension, fine, or loss of benefits.

To fix this some experts argue that a fundamental shift in leadership is needed. "The work that needs to be done certainly involves progressive leadership," said Thomas Nolan, a Boston police veteran and criminologist at Merrimack College of Massachusetts. "We've seen unfortunately, too little of that. We see the same types of people and there are exceptions being put in chief executive positions in police departments across the country."

Policing in America, particularly at the leadership level tends to be quite insular. For example, William Bratton served as the police commissioner in Boston in the early 1990s, commissioner in New York City in the mid-1990s, Chief of Police of Los Angeles in the 2000s, and finally as commissioner again in New York City from 2014 to 2016.

Anthony Batts similarly served as police chief in Oakland and Long Beach, California before moving to the Baltimore Police Department from 2012 to 2015. There are many more similar examples in big and medium size cities' police departments. If the same people tend to be in charge of police agencies, how can we expect them to change to be more transparent?

> **On-the-job incentives for police officers need to change**

As part of changing the culture of transparency and accountability several experts also argued that the incentives many police departments across the country impose on their officers need to change. The most commonly cited example comes from Ferguson, Missouri where Michael Brown's death by police in 2014, effectively launched the modern Black Lives Matter protests. The Justice Department investigated the Ferguson Police Department as a result of the protests. It found that police were encouraged to ticket as many people as possible with the explicit goal of raising as much revenue as possible from fines and fees. But to do this, police targeted the most vulnerable – mainly black residents with frivolous charges.

The Justice Department cited one example

Officers frequently arrest individuals under Section 29-16(1) on facts that do not meet the provision's elements. Section 29-16(1) makes it unlawful to "fail to comply with the lawful order or request of a police officer in the discharge of the officer's official duties where such failure interfered with, obstructed or hindered the officer in the performance of such duties." Many cases initiated under this provision begin with an officer ordering an individual to stop despite lacking evidence that the individual is engaged in wrong-doing. The order to stop is not a *lawful order* under those circumstances because the officer lacks reasonable suspicion that criminal activity is afoot. Nonetheless, when individuals do not stop in those situations, FPD (Ferguson Police Depart-ment) officers treat that conduct as a failure to comply with a lawful order and make arrests. This is not exclusive to Ferguson. In New York City, a group of police officers tried to sue the city and police department over a *quota* to stop and arrest as many people as possible. Some officers acknowl-edged that officers met this incentive by targeting low income black neighborhoods with little political power. "When you put any type of numbers on a police officer to perform we are going to go to the most vulnerable," Adhyl Polanco, one of the New York City police officers, told WNBC.

"We're going to the LGBT community, we're going to the black community and we're going to go to those people that have no boat, that have no power."

Experts say that police can still be incentivized for produc-tivity but that can be done without focusing so much on specific numbers of arrests or traffic tickets. It can be done in a more subjective manner through direct supervision.

It can also be coupled with other types of data, such as the number of complaints leveled at an officer and how many times a particular cop used force. But the bottom line is police need to be aware of how strict quotas and incentives can lead officers astray and take steps to correct any of those unwanted side effects.

> ## We need higher standards for police and better pay for cops

Who becomes a police officer likely needs to change, as well by setting a higher bar for who can qualify for the job? There are no federal standards for police officers. Federal lawmakers could establish such guidelines allowing states to treat them as the bare minimum or even expand on them. States could also individually up their licensing requirements for police. For example, in Florida, barbers are required under state law to have more training than police. Barbers need to log 1,200 hours while cops need 770. It's just one state but it exemplifies how poor the standards can be for police licensing across the US.

Then there are other considerations, such as whether cities and states should require a college degree for cops something that isn't required in much of the country right now. But generally, experts say there should be strong requirements in place that can check for the skills and characteristics we expect of police before they're put in a live situation. "We want to recruit people who have the capacity for emotional regulation so they don't get angry, they don't see authority challenges as personal challenges, they don't fall on the use of force as the first response to a challenge to their authority," said Jeffrey Fagan, a criminologist at Columbia University. "We want people who are good at planning and thinking ahead. We want people who have a capacity to reflect on their own work and learn from their mistakes."

But, Fagan added, "In order to do that, we need to think seriously about paying these guys better." This is the rub: higher standards will almost certainly lead to a need to pay cops more. Otherwise, why would someone with a college degree take a job as a police officer when he or she can get far more pay at a private security firm? John Roman, a criminal justice expert at the University of Chicago, agreed; "I think we should have higher standards. And if you're going to have higher standards, you're going to have to pay them better to attract better quality people. That's just the way the free market works," said Mr. Roman.

> **Police need to focus on the few people in communities causing chaos and violence**

Along with all these changes, police can also take steps that explicitly go after crime while limiting who's impacted by policing actions. The vast majority of crime in communities is perpetrated by just a few people in a few specific parts of the city.

As Abt, the Harvard criminologist, wrote for Vox, "In most cities across the nation, 3% - 5% of city blocks account for 50% - 75% of all shootings and killings, with 1% of a city's population responsible for 50% - 60% of all homicides." If police focus on just these few blocks specifically, individuals through policing strategies known as *hot spot* policing and focused deterrence, then they can deter a lot of crimes in their cities.

Focused deterrence in particular has been hugely successful. Study after study backs the data up and the method received much of the credit for the *Boston Miracle* that saw the city's violent crime rate drop by 79% in the 1990s. Professor Rosenfeld of the University of Missouri in St. Louis explained the two prongs of focused deterrence. "We clearly know who you are, where you live, and we're going to do everything we can to stop the violence in this community.

If that means that we arrest and charge you with a serious violent crime, we're going to do that. If you want out of this life, then here are services and support that you might find useful to set a different direction of your life."

The social services can be costly but they're needed for the strategy to work. For one, they offer a way out to someone caught in a bad place in life because people often get trapped in violent situations due to desperate economic situations. And when cops offer these services, they also signal that they're not just there to enforce the law but also to try to help people out of dire circumstances. "That lends a certain legitimacy to the police," Rosenfeld said. "They're not there to just serve warrants or warn people about what's going to happen to them if they commit another crime but also conveys a certain degree of concern for those individuals and their lives."

So these strategies can limit who's directly impacted by policing and by targeting a few people in a few areas instead of sweeping whole neighborhoods with aggressive stops. They can also signal to the community that the police get it. Most people in these communities are innocent and police are going to focus only on those who aren't. One big hurdle to these strategies is they can involve a big initial investment and police departments that are used to fighting crime in a certain way may be resistant to new ideas especially if they cost more money upfront. But if these strategies work to save and improve lives, there's a moral imperative for all levels of government to take them more seriously.

➢ We need better data to evaluate police and crime

If the federal government does get more involved in funding policing it could also stand to make another change which would massively improve the data collected on crime and policing in America. As it stands, the federal government does a terrible job collecting data on crime and police actions. Nationwide crime reports tend to come out with a nearly one-year lag period. And virtually every expert agrees that this data very likely undercounts crime since it misses crimes that aren't reported to the police. "We know virtually nothing about crime in America other than murder, kidnapping, and arson," Professor Roman of the University of Chicago said. "Rape, robbery, assault, motor vehicle theft, gangs and drugs are not reported back that allows the federal government to tell law enforcement how to behave more efficiently or helps researchers understand how crime is created and evolves."

But more comprehensive and current data could be very useful for fighting crime, several experts argued.

"You need that comparative information so you can determine whether that problem you're experiencing in your own community is relatively distinctive or specific to local community conditions or it's a common problem in many other communities," Rosenfeld said. "If it's the latter, you want to consult with those other communities to see how they're addressing it. If it's the former, then you know you have to devise strategies that respond to the specifics of the problems in your own community."

It's not just crime though. Goff pointed out that there's little to no data on what police do for such stops, arrests, use of force and so on. A 2015 study found that the federal agencies' police killing data misses as many as half of all people killed by police in America. And the federal government doesn't try to track more typical police actions from stops to arrests. The Justice Department is moving on a couple of initiatives to change this but they are still in very early stages, and it's unclear if the Trump administration will continue these efforts.

As long as America fails to collect this data, it's going to be impossible to evaluate what works to address virtually any of the issues people have with police such as racial bias to crime fighting. It may cost more money to collect this data properly, but every expert believes that this is a major issue that needs to be addressed. If police get this right they can boost faith in cops and their legitimacy in crime fighting. There's an underlying point in all of these strategies which is more effective and transparent policing really can solve the two big problems of racial bias and high crime pegged to police in America today.

Whenever another police shooting of a black man hits the news, opponents of Black Lives Matter tend to fall back on the question: *what about black-on-black crime?* The suggestion is that far more black people are murdered by black civilians and so that's really what someone worried about black lives should be concerned about? What these critics miss is that distrust in the police – the key driver behind Black Lives Matter is also a key driver of crime in minority neighborhoods. "When communities don't trust the police and are afraid of the police, then they will not and cannot work with police and within the law around issues in their own community," Professor Kennedy of John Jay College said. "Then those issues within the community become issues the community needs to deal with on their own and that leads to violence."

A study was particularly illuminating to this end. The study, from sociologists Matthew Desmond from Harvard, Andrew Papachristos of Yale, and David Kirk of Oxford looked at the effects of 911 calls in Milwaukee after incidents of police violence hit the news. They found that after the 2004 police beating of Frank Jude, 17% (22,200) fewer 911 calls were made in the following year compared with the number of calls that would have been made had the Frank Jude beating never happened.

More than half of the effect came from fewer calls in black neighborhoods. And the effect persisted for more than a year, even after the officers involved in the beating were punished. Researchers found similar impacts on local 911 calls after other high-profile incidents of police violence. But crime was still happening in these neighborhoods.

Indeed, as 911 calls dropped, researchers also found a rise in homicides. They note that the spring and summer that followed Jude's story were the deadliest in the seven years observed.

That suggests that people were simply dealing with crime themselves. And although the researchers couldn't definitively prove it, that might mean civilians took to their own devices. Sometimes violence means to protect themselves when they couldn't trust police to stop crime and violence.

An important implication of this finding is that publicized cases of police violence not only threaten the legitimacy and reputation of law enforcement, the researchers write, they also by driving down 911 calls thwart the suppression of law breaking, obstruct the application of justice and ultimately make cities as a whole and the black community in particular, less safe.

Better policing can't stop all crime. There are many other issues that need to be addressed such as jobs, economic stability, education and housing also have an impact. But if police were trusted by the community it can have a sizable effect. To some degree, this should be common sense. Journalist Jill Leovy captured it well in her brilliant book, *Ghettoside*. Noting that homicides are much less likely to be solved in black neighborhoods with a trusted alliance between the black community and police. She argues that some people in black communities have concluded that police don't value black lives and so they need to settle interpersonal conflicts on their own.

Leovy writes, "Take a bunch of teenage boys from the whitest, safest suburb in America and plunk them down in a place where their friends are murdered and they are constantly attacked and threatened. Signal that no one cares and fail to solve murders. Limit their options for escape. Then see what happens." That's why transparency, accountability, and community cooperation, described as part of the *procedural justice* model of policing are all so important. They signal that the justice system does care.

In conclusion, as a black man, I understand the frustrations of racism and police brutality that's escalated to epic proportion. We must address this issue that's plagued African Americans since 1852 – the creation and structural racism of police departments throughout the United States. We must create polices in which CORRUPT law enforcement learn TRUE justice!

– Police didn't have to murder George Floyd!

– Police didn't have to murder Botham Jean!

– Police didn't have to murder Breonna Taylor!

– Police didn't have to murder Sandra Bland!

– Police didn't have to murder Tamir Rice!

– Police didn't have to murder Eric Garner!

– Police didn't have to murder Mike Brown!

– Police didn't have to murder Freddie Gray!

V.

Racism and the Trump Presidency

In 2020, public poll numbers have painted an unflattering picture for Trump. Poll after poll has shown him down to Biden (2020 Democratic nominee for president) nationally by sizable margins, and struggling in key states that will decide the elections. Another sign: a New York Times-Siena College poll that showed Biden's strength across key demographic groups – and a 61% disapproval of Trump's handling of race relations in the aftermath of George Floyd's death while in police custody in Minneapolis.

When protests broke out at the end of May 2020 following Floyd's death, (George Floyd was murdered by police officers with a knee on his neck while on the ground face down) some of Trump's advisers encouraged him to adopt a more unifying tone amid a national reckoning on race, even as the President pushed a hard-line "law and order" stance he believed would play better with his voters.

Aides made various attempts to bring the issues facing Black Americans directly before Trump, including some advisers who relayed stories of racism they had heard from friends, roundtables with Black community leaders and a session with families who had lost loved ones to police violence.

Yet people close to the President say he hasn't appeared to internalize or accept the descriptions of systemic racism that are now being examined and called out in a national racial reckoning. Asked in a Wall Street Journal interview whether he believed systemic racism exists, Trump said: "I'd like to think there is not but unfortunately, there probably is some. I would also say it's very substantially less than it used to be."

Instead of seeking a unifying tone, Trump has retrenched into the divisive themes he believes are the not-so-secret ingredient to his political success thus far. A successive series of advisers have encouraged a bigger approach they believe more befits an incumbent President. But Trump has resisted, unwilling or unable to move past the rhetoric he insists is a political winner.

That the current tumult over race coincides with troubling news for his reelection prospects including sinking poll numbers and a disappointing foray onto the campaign trail last weekend in Tulsa, where he kicked off his reelection campaign much to the anger of African Americans on Juneteenth weekend only sharpened the impression of Trump reaching for racially divisive language and messages as both a political life jacket and a personal security blanket. From supporting confederate monuments to re-tweeting a video of supporter yelling, "White Power," to his attacks on his predecessor Barack Obama, which began with his promotion of the racist "birther" conspiracy 10 years ago, which continues today. He calls NFL players "sons of bitches" and suggested they are un-American even as their kneeling protests seek to highlight police brutality.

Trump has openly used imagery and descriptions of police tactics that hearken to the violence during the Civil Rights era, including descriptions of "vicious dogs." He tweeted a phrase, "when the looting starts, shooting starts," that originated in the 1960s with a police chief in Miami accused of racism.

And while Trump has stressed the importance of preserving the nation's history and "heritage" as he takes steps to prevent the destruction of Confederate monuments and symbols, he did not acknowledge the racist violence that took place in Tulsa 99 years ago when he visited the city for a campaign rally the day after Juneteenth. Trump continues to leave no room for doubt that he's a bona fide racist. However, Trump supporters don't view him as a racist. So let us explore further the question that many of us already know but others are still find it difficult to accept – **Is Donald Trump a racist?**

Behind that question lies a still more important one: *How should we define the term racism?* There are at least two main ways of defining racism. The most popular definition of racism is racial prejudice. By this definition, racism is a personal and moral failure. Many social scientists study racism this way. Concepts like *old-fashioned racism* (thinking African Americans are inherently inferior to whites) or *racial resentment* (thinking that African Americans are culturally inferior to whites) think of racism as rooted in the individual. The other way is to see racism specifically since the mid-20th century as a system of discrimination. In this view, a person does not need to be full of hate to perpetuate racism. Under this broader definition of racism it is a means to an end. This definition is founded on the concept that race was socially constructed to divide, dehumanize and maintain power.

Despite decades of history indicating that race is socially constructed to obtain and keep power, the popularity of the individual based understanding of racism leads people to look for someone to blame for the persistent discrimination black people experience. One reason we keep asking, *Is [fill in the blank] racist?* Maybe that humans automatically attribute one's actions to personal flaws rather than considering social factors that may contribute. This tendency is so common it is called the *fundamental attribution error* and it's why the person who cuts you off on the road is a jerk and why when you do the same thing, it's because you're in a hurry. At one level, it is comforting to believe that individual racists are responsible for the evil in the world. After all, if we could get rid of these racists or change their minds we would have the equality so often invoked by quoting the Rev. Martin Luther King Jr.'s "I Have a Dream" speech. Under the individual actor interpretation of racism, calling someone a racist is a moral indictment of the person's character. One example is Roseanne Barr's firing from her television show after making a racist joke on Twitter. The moral weight of labeling someone a racist justifies their punishment and theoretically, discourages racist behavior.

Trump's only election strategy was racism and he knew it would turn out his base and even swung some independents over to his side. Racial fear proved to be a valuable ally to Trump. According to Gallup polling in October 2018, immigration ranked as the second most important issue for Republicans, just a hair behind the economy, and second highest for all eligible voters.

It's a strategy deliberately crafted to drive a wedge right into the immigrant community itself with some older immigrants standing with the president against undocumented workers and some Asian Americans siding with the Republican Party on its anti-Affirmative Action stance. But at the time Trump wasn't thinking just about the midterm elections.

Trump's goal is to continue to create an atmosphere of chaos and panic that allows him to act more forcefully speak more rashly and present himself as the country's savior. He's a grandstanding nationalist who has finally found his calling which is to preserve white dominance in the United States and prevent the country from becoming part of a multi-cultural world.

On the morning after a unique wave of despair, anger, fear and depression washed over much of black America. After learning that Donald Trump had been elected president, some folks cried, sought refuge in the Bible and comforted frightened children. Others steeled themselves for life under a president who has re-tweeted white supremacists, promised to increase stop-and-frisk policing in poor black neighborhoods, falsely connected Mexican immigrants to crime, and launched his political brand by attacking the legitimacy of the first black president's birth certificate. Plenty of white Hillary Clinton supporters also felt strong emotions after Trump's victory. But his track record on race seemed to make his triumph cut deeper and feel more personal to many African Americans. One sentiment rang loudest in many African American hearts and minds: the election shows where we really stand. Now the truth is plain to see that an uncomfortable percentage of white people view the concerns and lives of their black fellow citizens.

"Transparency is the order of the day. Now we see what was hidden," said Melvin Steals, a retired teacher and principal who lives in the western Pennsylvania town of Baden. Fifty-seven percent of his county, a mix of rural areas and hollowed-out towns, voted for Trump. "It's like the era after

Reconstruction all over again, when they wanted to eradicate all of the gains made by blacks after the Civil War," Steals said. After the war that ended slavery, an activist federal government helped the south's newly freed African Americans gain a hold in society and elected offices before a racist backlash firmly restored white supremacy. "This is another opportunity to reassert their authority," said Steals.

At the core there is something nefarious about it. It's tied into white supremacy, that it's their way or the highway. According to exit polls, Trump won the votes of 67% of whites without a college degree, the bedrock of his support. He captured 58% of the total white vote, and beat Clinton 49% to 45% among white college graduates. Fifty-four percent of white male college graduates voted for Trump. Trump did make overtures to the black community, promising to bring jobs and better education to struggling cities. Eight percent of black voters chose Trump, better than GOP presidential nominee Mitt Romney, who got 7% against President Barack Obama in 2012. Among Latinos, 29% backed Trump, more than Romney's 27%

In 2007, in the early days of Obama's first presidential campaign, there was widespread disbelief among African Americans that many white people would vote for a black man.

A majority of black folks essentially overestimated the extent of white racism. "Obama would need 43% of the white vote in some states to win, and that's humanly impossible," said one South Carolina lawmaker at the time. Yet in 2008, Obama won 43% of the white vote nationally – more than previous Democratic candidates John Kerry and Al Gore.

"I was one of those people who thought this ain't gonna happen. White people won't elect a black president," said

Eric Woods, a 47-year-old consultant in Boston. Now, he believes Trump's election was a reversion to the mean. "I think white working class people who have seen their economic and social capital diminish sent a message: This guy is saying we can have our heyday again."

What does it mean that so many whites voted for someone whom so many others viewed as racist? In a widely shared interpretation, CNN commentator Van Jones called the results, "A whitelash against a changing country." "We don't want to feel that someone has been elected by throwing away some of us to appeal more deeply to others. This is a deeply painful moment," Jones said.

Trump was masterful in tapping in on a perception that people of color are causing working-class people's pain. So whether it's in the package of immigration or in the package of black lazy folks or the package of Mexicans that scapegoat, he's able to tap in on that. The feelings of sorrow and betrayal also stemmed from how white Trump voters regard racism and oppression. They're not taking it seriously because they don't view it as legitimate. "It's not real," said Jean-Max Hogarth, a 49-year-old physician from Maryland, also confronted tears the morning after. His 18-year-old daughter, who had voted for the first time came into his bedroom at 4:30 a.m. crying hysterically. She said, "I'm really afraid for my future," Hogarth said. She also said, "She couldn't believe her fellow Americans voted for a person like that, a man she doesn't believe represents America." She couldn't believe that the KKK won – that their interests won. Trump created his political popularity by using racist techniques of the birther issue and he never apologized. Trump's unwillingness to denounce the KKK is nothing more than his attempt to appeal to the worst of the American nature; that racism is the original sin of America. Trump has tapped into the very thing that has historically prevented African Americans and poor whites from really understanding their similar needs and interests. They are beginning to understand the level of racism this man displays.

Some African Americans believed the nature of their daily interactions with white people would change. Cameron White, a 26-year-old product designer in Austin, Texas, said he had been praying and seeking his father's advice. "Being in Texas, knowing this state voted for him, I'm wondering if I'm talking to people who are secretly hating me on the inside." "It's hard for me to look a white person in the face right now," said Drew Schifino, a 35-year-old basketball coach from Pittsburgh. He said, "I woke up depressed." "I just don't understand how they could vote for a dude like that." But as reality set in and the shock and pain began to ebb, many glimpsed another chapter of the African-American struggle against a bias that never seems to lose its bite.

Former Cleveland Cavalier and current Los Angeles Laker, LeBron James, posted a message on Instagram shortly after the election of Trump that said, in part: "Minorities and women in all please know that this isn't the end, it's just a very challenging obstacle that we will overcome!! The Man above will never put something in our paths that we can't handle no matter how difficult it may feel/be!" Steals came to a similar place; "It's taken me 70 years to find the courage that Martin Luther King had," he said. "Courage is going forward in spite of your fear."

So, is Trump racist? Wading into a racially charged case from his past, Donald Trump indicated that the *Central Park Five*; consisting of young African American and Latino teens were guilty despite being officially exonerated by DNA evidence decades after the notorious 1989 rape case in New York.

"They admitted they were guilty," Trump said to CNN in a statement. "The police doing the original investigation say they were guilty. The fact that that case was settled with so much evidence against them is outrageous. And the woman, so badly injured, will never be the same." The five men were convicted as teenagers after implicating each other under intense questioning over a brutal sexual assault on a jogger that dominated the tabloids. Defenders said they were coerced into confessing and all five were later cleared by DNA evidence and a separate confession in 2002 from another criminal who took credit for the assault. New York eventually paid them $41 million in a settlement in 2014 over their ordeal.

Trump had taken out a full-page ad at the time of the crime calling for New York to reinstate the death penalty in response. The case was notable for its racial politics: Four of the Central Park Five were black and one was Latino while the victim was a white banker. During the 2016 presidential campaign, Hillary Clinton's campaign denounced Trump's statements. "The facts here are clear. These men were exonerated. Another man has admitted to committing the crime as proven by DNA evidence," the campaign said in a statement. Trump rushed to judgment on the case, has refused to admit he is wrong and continues to peddle yet another racist lie, a pattern for him and a clear reason why he is unfit to be president.

Donald Trump *is* racist? However, if you ask Trump, he'll tell that he isn't racist. To the contrary, he's repeatedly said that he's "The least racist person that you've ever encountered." Trump's actual record though, tells a very different story. In July 2019, Trump tweeted that several black and brown members of Congress are "From countries whose governments are a complete and total catastrophe" and that they should "Go back to those countries." The tweets, aimed at Reps. Alexandria Ocasio-Cortez (D-NY), Ayanna Pressley (D-MA), Ilhan Omar (D-MN), and Rashida Tlaib (D-MI), exemplify a common racist trope used against immigrants and minority groups who criticize U.S. policies. Democrats, including House Speaker Nancy Pelosi, condemned Trump's tweets as racist.

This is nothing new for Trump. In fact, the very first time that Trump appeared in the pages of the New York Times, back in the 1970s, was when the U.S. Department of Justice sued him for racial discrimination. Since then, he has repeatedly appeared in newspaper pages across the world as he inspired similar controversies.

This long history is important. It would be one thing if Trump simply misspoke one or two times. But when you take all of Trump's actions and comments together, a clear pattern emerges – one that suggests that bigotry is not just political opportunism on Trump's part but a real element of Trump's personality, character, and career.

The evidence is there like a smoking gun that he has a great deal of racial stereotypes and downright bigoted views of black people and other people of color. The evidence also reveals a complexity and pervasiveness to racism that disadvantage black Americans cannot be reduced to a single person or undone by eliminating individual bias. There are many Donald Trumps in America and they are no longer hiding their views.

VI.

The Media and Racism

In 2020, tensions inside American newsrooms have emerged amid the protests over the killings and shootings of George Floyd while in police custody, Breonna Taylor, Jacob Blake and other black people and people of color including clashes between reporters and editors and concerns about newsroom diversity. While 2020 studies shows black Americans give high marks to the news media's coverage of the protests, a survey conducted before the protests found deep divides between racial and ethnic groups in feelings of how the news media represent them.

While most Americans say that the news media do not understand them, black, Hispanic and white Americans often cite very different reasons for why they are misunderstood, according to a Pew Research Center survey conducted Feb. 18-March 2, 2020.

Majority of Americans say news organizations don't understand them

% of U.S. adults who say news organizations ...

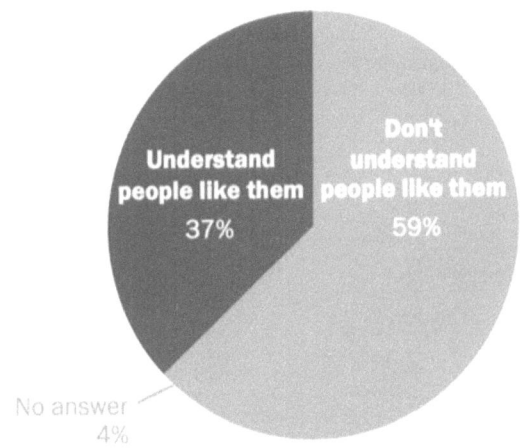

Source: Survey of U.S. adults conducted Feb. 18-March 2, 2020.

PEW RESEARCH CENTER

Overall, 59% of Americans think news organizations do not understand people like them, while a minority – 37% – say they do feel understood. This feeling is about on par with the last time the question was asked in 2018. While no one reason dominates when looking at all Americans, sizable gaps exist between racial and ethnic groups in why they feel misunderstood. Roughly similar portions of black (58%), Hispanic (55%) and white Americans (61%) say the news media misunderstand them, but they cite markedly different reasons for this misunderstanding.

Black Americans are far more likely than the other two groups to feel that the misunderstanding is based on their race or some other demographic trait. Among black adults who think the news media do not understand people like them, about a third (34%) say the main way they are misunderstood is their personal characteristics. This is far higher than the 10% of white adults and 17% of Hispanic adults who say the same.

Black, white and Hispanic Americans give very different reasons for why they feel the news media don't understand them

Among U.S. adults who say news organizations do not understand people like them, % who say ___ is what news organizations misunderstand the most about them

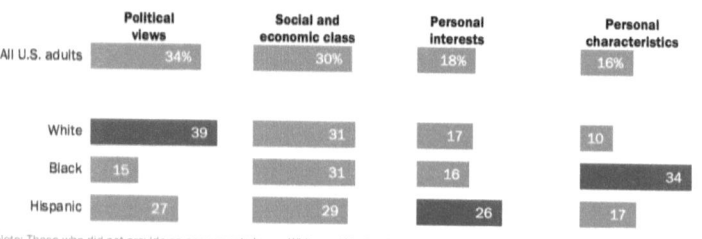

Note: Those who did not provide an answer not shown. White and black adults include those who report being only one race and are non-Hispanic. Hispanics are of any race.
Source: Survey of U.S. adults conducted Feb. 18-March 2, 2020.
PEW RESEARCH CENTER

White Americans, on the other hand, are far more likely than the other groups to say the problem stems from political misunderstandings. Of white adults who say news organizations misunderstand them, nearly four-in-ten (39%) say it's mostly based on their political views. About a quarter of Hispanic Americans say the same, and both groups are higher than black Americans (15%).

Hispanic Americans are somewhat more likely than the other two groups to think that their personal interests are what is misunderstood most (26%, compared with 16% of black and 17% of white adults). In a 2019 study, U.S. adults living in areas with a higher proportion of Hispanic residents were somewhat less likely to feel a connection to local journalists and news organizations, such as through speaking to a journalist.

All three racial or ethnic groups are about on par in thinking that the news media misunderstand their social and economic class.

A similar question was posed to those who feel the news media do understand them, asking how they are most understood, and again, no single reason dominates. (For more details, you can find a link to the questions and responses in "How we did this"). But on this question, the divides by race and ethnicity are often not nearly as large.

Divides do emerge between political parties and other demographic groups in whether they feel news organizations understand them. For instance, Republicans and Republican-leaning independents are far more likely to feel the news media misunderstand them than Democrats and Democratic leaners (73% vs. 47%). Male U.S. adults are somewhat more likely than female adults to feel this, and those ages 18 to 29 are more likely to say this than those older than them.

Divides between the parties and demographic groups also emerge when it comes to why they feel misunderstood, though these divides are often not as large as by race and ethnicity, particularly when it comes to the feeling that their personal characteristics are misunderstood.

Differences emerge between demographic groups in why they feel the news media misunderstand them

Among U.S. adults who think news organizations do not understand people like them, % of who say ___ is what news organizations misunderstand the most about them

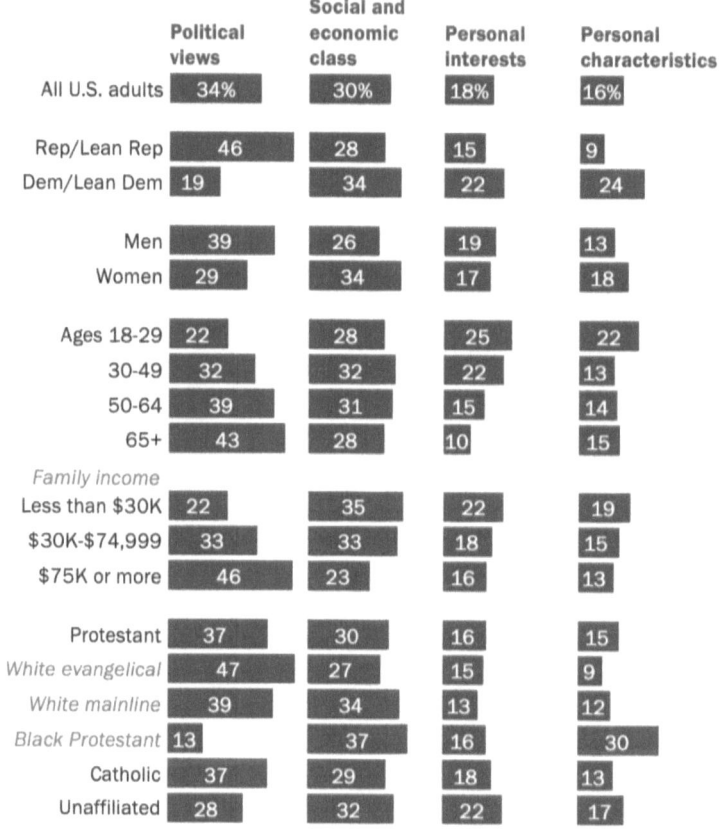

	Political views	Social and economic class	Personal interests	Personal characteristics
All U.S. adults	34%	30%	18%	16%
Rep/Lean Rep	46	28	15	9
Dem/Lean Dem	19	34	22	24
Men	39	26	19	13
Women	29	34	17	18
Ages 18-29	22	28	25	22
30-49	32	32	22	13
50-64	39	31	15	14
65+	43	28	10	15
Family income				
Less than $30K	22	35	22	19
$30K-$74,999	33	33	18	15
$75K or more	46	23	16	13
Protestant	37	30	16	15
White evangelical	47	27	15	9
White mainline	39	34	13	12
Black Protestant	13	37	16	30
Catholic	37	29	18	13
Unaffiliated	28	32	22	17

Note: For statistical differences between groups, please ask Pew Research Center. Those who did not provide an answer not shown.
Source: Survey of U.S. adults conducted Feb. 18-March 2, 2020.

PEW RESEARCH CENTER

For instance, Republicans who feel news organizations misunderstand them are far more likely to say their political views are most misunderstood, while Democrats are somewhat more likely to cite their social class, personal interests and personal characteristics.

Americans 50 years of age and older are more likely to cite their political views, while those younger than that are more likely to think their personal interests are misunderstood. Those with a household income of $75,000 or higher are less likely to cite social class, but more likely to say political views than those with a lower household income.

The growth of racism during the past few years has been paralleled by a radical shift in the terms of debate on strategies for defeating it. In the early 1970s, minority actions by the far left against the national front were condemned in hysterical terms by commentators and politicians whose line for defeating racists was 'ignore them and they'll go away. Today, battle lines of moderates spar with each other in denouncing racism and bigotry. A similar change in attitudes has occurred in mass media. Early in the decade proprietors, editors and journalists would deny the possibility of any link between the media's output and the growth of racism in the streets. But in recent times a number of articles and pamphlets have been written which attack with varying degrees of ferocity the role played by the media at least in reinforcing and often in actively promoting racism. For the media and the politicians, this change of heart on racism entails severe problems and contradictions.

It is becoming difficult to reconcile opposition to racism with a record of vindictive legislation against black people in particular and of a pro-capitalist austerity program in general. The media face a similar predicament since by beginning to accept some responsibility for the content and effects of their output they begin to explore the notions of balance and impartiality which form the cornerstone of their ideological potency. Anti-racists therefore have an excellent opportunity to hone in on these contradictions and transform posturing against racism into effective opposition.

The notion that black people are collectively and almost by definition, a problem for society is basic to most media output. Black people are muggers, scroungers, illegal immigrants, dope-crazed, any variety of misfits. Black people above all are portrayed as different. Usually reported in a negative context as an aspect of a supposedly collective problem. African Americans seldom get the opportunity to express their own point of view. Black people who do get the chance to speak out can usually be counted on to articulate essentially white middle class values and aspirations, threatening nobody but saying even less about the true situation of the black community. Even black people who are successful or famous remain *black* by society. News channels and online outlets are used as a source for people to find out about what is currently happening in America or around the rest of the world. The main aim is to service the public by bringing people awareness on certain situations from an impartial standpoint. However, this is not always the case especially concerning black people.

The first example would be the perception of black men through news outlets. Looking at America specifically over the past few years we've seen and heard of many shootings by police of young black boys. Many of them were caused based off of the negative associations that people have towards black men. One example would be Trayvon Martin, a 17 year old teen who was killed by George Zimmerman, a neighborhood watch volunteer.

In George Zimmerman's allegations for what Trayvon did to cause him to shoot him, words like he looked *suspicious* because he was wearing a hoodie or *he was going to become violent* after George Zimmerman approached him only presents what Trayvon didn't do but how George Zimmerman assumed he would act based off of assumptions, possibly caused by Trayvon's race.

The news played a part in this when photos where displayed of both George Zimmerman and Trayvon Martin. For Zimmerman the media used photos of him in color, smiling and giving the appearance of a happy or friendly person. However, for Martin, the murdered victim, the media used photos of him wearing a hoodie, frowning, looking unapproachable and in black and white making his face appear harsher as if he wasn't a good person.

Many people became angered about this, as on the internet there where many other photos available that they could've used of Martin where he is smiling and would have been depicted similar to Zimmerman's own photo. So it leaves the question: *why would news outlets purposely use that photo of Martin when there were many more available?*

Most African American men today lead difficult lives due to the negative public perceptions that they've been associated with for decades. Even when walking outside they are regularly treated by police as dangerous suspects when they haven't done anything wrong. Again, the police behavior is just based off of assumptions. Due to the psychological affect this has on the way the public perceives African American men when applying for jobs and in some instances, the majority are turned away and only given the reason that they're not "the right fit" for that work place when in actuality it's because these employers are expecting them to behave or appear a certain way based only on their race.

Charleston church shooter Dylann Roof was loner caught in 'Internet evil,' family says nbcnews.tc/1dWf6BA

Son with troubled past shields mom from gunfire, dies saving her in South Chicago: chicago.suntimes.com/news/7771/7976...

Black men are not the only victims as to how the media presents their ideals. African American families are also misinterpreted. In America, if one was to rely solely on what national news outlets reported about African American families, you'd walk away thinking that many of them are *overwhelmingly poor, reliant on welfare, absentee fathers* and *criminals.*

A study by Dr. Travis L Dixon showed that major news outlets routinely present a distorted picture of black families purposely portraying them as dependent and dysfunctional people with the idea that all black people are incapable of taking care of themselves and consumed by family instability which is the reason for all their problems.

Through previous research we've seen how black people have created or encouraged negative depictions of ourselves through hip hop with the association of being violent and using profanities and slang where people think we appear uneducated. However, with the news we see how non-black people in charge of a wider audience also aid these stereotypes and the negative effects it has on black men and black families. This isn't the first time where characteristics such as being poor or complacent has been associated with black people throughout my research. But it is the first time where black people have been portrayed unfairly concerning the images used for Trayvon Martin and other similar cases as it appears these are the only depictions of black people the media wants to present and the way they want the public to view African Americans.

Obviously this has an extremely negative impact on black people and as presented earlier, depicts how it affects black men looking for jobs, and how the public view black families. When having only these portrayals, society will view African Americans in this manner.

The Media Portrayal of Black Families v White Families

There is a stark difference in how the media portrays black and white families. According to a study by the nonprofit civil rights advocacy group, Color of Change, an organization that advocates for families which looked at more than 800 local and national US news stories and opinion pieces between January 2015 and December 2016. The media overwhelmingly depicted black families as poor and dependent on welfare, black fathers as absent and consistently overinflated the link between black families and criminality. However, when it comes to white families, the picture painted is often of social stability.

In America, African American families represent 59% of the poor in the media but make up just 27% of the poor of the general population, says the study. White families, on the other hand, represent 17% of the poor in media, but make up 66% of the poor across the country. The report notes that since the 1980s, conservatives racked up attacks against so-called "welfare queens" – a stereotype that presents black women as having children in order to receive bountiful welfare assistance from the government. Researchers concluded that such portrayals were rife in the media and led to the perception that black people not only benefited the most from government aid but were also far more likely to cheat the system than white people. This is despite the fact that white working families are the biggest beneficiaries of welfare. In 2014, government assistance and tax credits lifted 6.2 million working class whites out of poverty; more than any other racial group.

The study also analyzed the depiction of black fathers. Media reports suggest black men often abandon their children and families though there's no evidence they do so at higher rates than white fathers.

The misrepresentation of black fathers as *absentee* stems in part from the common but incorrect use of non-marital birthrates as a proxy for parental involvement and falsely leading to the assumption that black fathers who are not married to the mothers of their children must not be involved parents.

A 2013 and 2018 report conducted by the Center for Disease Control found that black fathers were more likely to have bathed, dressed or helped their children use the toilet every day compared with white fathers. Black fathers were more likely to take their children to or from activities every day compared with white fathers and a larger percentage of black fathers helped their children with homework every day in the last four weeks compared with white fathers.

The study also found that the media overrepresented the link between black families and criminality and underrepresented it for white families. Researchers pointed out that black family members represented 37% of criminals in the media but made up 26% of family members arrested for criminal activity according to crime reports. White families represented 28% of criminals in the media but made up 77% of those arrested for criminal activity.

For years, the media have been criticized for their representations of African Americans on television.

Communication research and theory suggest that the mass media are an important source of information about African Americans and media portrayals contribute to public perceptions of African Americans for example, has argued that images on television may cause viewers to conceive, alter, or even reinforce their negative beliefs and opinions about African American families.

The racial stereotypes of early American history had a significant role in shaping attitudes toward African-Americans during that time. Images of the Sambo, Jim Crow, the Savage, Mammy, Aunt Jemima, Sapphire, and Jezebel may not be as powerful today, yet they are still alive.

In conclusion, it is imperative that more African American journalists are needed in the newsroom to balance the scales of fair and accurate journalism to help set a better standard to reach out to black experts and in doing so, will provide a more accurate, social and historical narrative.

VII.

Liberalism and the Issues of Racism

Since the election of President Donald Trump, there's been a lot of talk about how demographic changes and the prospect of racial equality, have left his strongest supporters fearful of losing *their* America which they see as a largely white nation. Yet commentators have paid less attention to the fact that many white American liberals harbor some of these same racial fears; a fear of not being part of the majority and a fear of losing the privileges they were born with.

Fundamentally, racist ideals are not the exclusive province of the right. A Reuter's poll during the 2016 election found that over 30% of Trump voters believed black people to be less intelligent than white people. But the same poll found that over 20% of Hillary Clinton voters felt the same way. Racism can be found across the political spectrum, and there is a long history of white liberals preaching equality while being reluctant to fully embrace efforts to make society more equal in ways that might discomfort them even a little. People born with privilege and power are often squeamish about giving any of it away. Joe Feagin, distinguished professor of sociology at Texas A&M University, says, "That white liberals are good on certain racial issues but often don't put a lot of action behind their words or don't go as far as they could to make racial equality a reality."

Feagin recounts a story about President Lyndon B. Johnson that illustrates his point. Johnson was responsible for getting three major civil rights laws passed during his presidency but was still leery of fully embracing the fight for equality. During the 1968 presidential campaign, while Johnson was still in the race, he created what was called the Kerner Commission to investigate why black Americans were rioting in cities around the country. In the end, the commission concluded that poverty and white racism were the causes. Upon seeing the results of his own commission, Johnson backed away from the report and even aspersed its findings. "That was the only commission in U.S. history which used language about white racism being the problem with race in this country," Feagin said. President Johnson saw the report and knew it was political dynamite during his 1968 run for president and backed off and attacked his own commission.

When it came down to it, Johnson prioritized the delicate feelings of white Americans over the needs of black Americans. He chose to appease white voters rather than confront the monumental problem of systemic racism. This isn't ancient history, though. Many modern politicians have a history of failing to support racial equality. Former Vice President Joe Biden now the Democratic presidential nominee for 2020, fought against racial integration efforts in the 1970s. Between 1973 and 1975, Biden regularly voted for proposals that aimed to prevent school districts from busing white and black students to different neighborhoods to create schools that were more equally mixed. Biden claimed he was in support of school integration, though he was anti-busing, says Jason Sokol, an associate professor of history at the University of New Hampshire. "Biden opposed the means that would achieve the end of school integration." Sokol said, "Biden did so because he feared losing the support of white Democrats who largely opposed these desegregation proposals."

In the 1990s, the Clinton administration helped pass a crime bill that many critics argued disproportionately targeted people of color and contributed to America's ongoing mass incarceration problem. Clinton signed the law at least in part to appeal to white voters afraid of minorities. Critics have also argued that the welfare reforms passed during the Clinton years were similarly based on the era's racist sentiments and have disproportionately harmed people of color. This historical baggage inevitably became something of a problem for Hilary Clinton during her 2016 presidential candidacy that she had to address during her campaign. She eventually said that parts of the Crime Bill had been "A mistake."

Over the past half-century, liberals have fought for racial equality and inclusivity on some occasions while standing in its way on others. Feagin argues that the reason for this apparent inconsistency is that white liberals often prefer to address racial inequality at a slow pace, in an effort to maintain something fairly close to the comfortable status quo. Further, Feagin said, "Many liberals often only want to address racism when they see a personal benefit to doing so. Once people get wealth and privilege, at least a majority of them don't want to give it up unless they can see a good reason for it."

Feagin points out that in the 1950s and early '60s, while the U.S. was in the midst of both the Cold War and the Jim Crow era, Soviets often used racial strife in the states for their international propaganda efforts. He recounts that when dogs were biting demonstrators in Birmingham, Alabama in the summer of 1963, the Soviet Union made thousands of photos of the incidents available across the planet. Essentially, the racial struggles in the south were giving the U.S. government a bad image internationally. In response, Feagin said, "The moderate to the liberal wing of the white male elite started to turn against segregation."

"The U.S. State Department which had been fairly conservative started issuing memos to the Supreme Court supporting school desegregation and supporting ending racial segregation in the South," Feagin stated. This style of treating racial justice as political rather than moral calculation is still in vogue in 2020. According to Feagin, contemporary white Democratic candidates will often push for policies that will increase racial equality but only so far as white moderates and white conservatives will let them. Politicians often attempt to weigh what voters of color want against what white people currently think is an acceptable amount of change in the power balance.

Feagin said, "There's a fair amount of support right now for going ahead with a federal commission to study reparations for black Americans. It's one thing to appoint a commission but it's another thing to actually support legislation and work for it." In the 2020 presidential campaign, white candidates danced around certain racial justice issues that white Americans see as radical. White Americans on the left and right often fear full racial equality and demographic change because of an implicit desire to maintain their present advantages. "On some level, we all want to belong to groups that confer advantage and give us a sense of stability and certainty. This is part of human nature," says Eric Knowles, associate professor of psychology at New York University.

And, in fact, studies suggest that white Americans from across the political spectrum may feel threatened by the prospect of becoming a minority.

Christopher Parker, professor of political science at the University of Washington, says that while conservative whites are more sensitive to a perceived loss of power, many liberals also worry about it. "Insights from behavioral economics suggest that most people, regardless of political orientation, are sensitive to perceived losses," Parker says. In polls, you'll find that white Americans of all backgrounds often voice concerns about possibly being discriminated against if they are no longer part of the ethnic majority. This concern would suggest that white Americans are aware on some level of how oppressive the white majority has been against people of color.

Yet Feagin says his research has not found that people of color actually have any desire for the kind of retribution that white Americans so fear. "When we conceive of ethnic *others* as a monolithic bloc, we tend to develop almost paranoiac theories about their intentions," Knowles says. There is also evidence that white Americans who oppose things like Affirmative Action are often against it not merely out of self-interest, but also because they're concerned with protecting the interests of other whites. "Many white liberals might support Affirmative Action in the abstract but worry that such programs contradict their own sense of meritocracy and might harm their own children's chances of getting into a good college," says Lily Geismer, associate professor of history at Claremont McKenna College.

This fear gets to the core of the hypocrisy of many white liberals. In the abstract, white liberals will say they want equality but when things get specific they're sometimes worried about losing what they've been handed and especially about being treated as badly as minorities in America have been treated in the past. Elijah Anderson, professor of sociology and African American studies at Yale University says that people on the left and people on the right often share the same fears when it comes to racial equality and demographic changes. "It's a human issue," Anderson says. "It's not a political issue whether you feel the fear. It's a political issue when you try to think about doing something about it."

In a piece for Vox in 2018, Anderson pointed out that white people of all backgrounds often feel uncomfortable with seeing people of color in *white spaces*, whether they realize it or not, from neighborhoods to business settings. We may have pushed desegregation in our laws, but it's clear many white Americans still haven't fully embraced a desegregated society in their minds.

While many Trump supporters and other white conservatives who hold similar ideals will explicitly oppose efforts to make society more racially equal and inclusive, many white liberals show more implicit biases that can harm efforts to achieve these goals. This does not mean that both sides are equally guilty when it comes to stalling such efforts, but it means that many of the people ostensibly fighting for anti-racist policies have some introspection to do. An ally is only as useful as their investment in the cause.

According to George Sachs, PsyD, clinical child psychologist and founder of the Sachs Center for ADD/ADHD and Asperger's in Manhattan, and guest writer for the Huffington Post (*10 Ways White Liberals Perpetuate Racism*, 2017) said, "Racism just won't die because its roots are deep. In a place where we don't like to go, racism is not only alive but thriving. It's automatic and hidden." Binding and resistant to change. Like the root kit on a computer, racism is hidden and operating without our knowledge. Too often these micro aggressions, in particular micro invalidations, go unchallenged by people of color, due to the inherent power imbalance felt with white people. Racism is experienced but not acknowledged.

When a person of color does take issue with those types of encounters, many well-meaning white liberals can become overly apologetic, defensive, or even offended when confronted with the subtle indignity of their words or actions. These knee-jerk defenses are actually how white liberals end up perpetuating racism. Thus, true self-awareness and deeper relationships with people of color never really happen. This is what young people know instinctively. And what older white liberals have a hard time understanding. Like it or not white superiority is well defended and protected. It may be unintentional and likely unconscious. Without more introspection and sincere interaction the racism train keeps rolling.

Right now some might feel angry and misjudged. Maybe white liberals are shaking their head, feeling slighted and angered by the lack of acknowledgement regarding their efforts and accomplishments concerning racial sensitivity. After all, white liberals are the white folks who really get it. Right? This is in fact, another micro invalidation. This particular micro aggression is called *attack by racial resume.* Some white liberals say, *look at all the work I've done on behalf of people of color. I'm one of the good ones!*

The following are 10 ways white liberals engage in subtle racism:

1. Denial:

"But I don't even see color."

Denying they could ever have racist thoughts or that they reap the benefits as a member of the majority race is a common defense of liberal white Americans. By denying the existence of racist thoughts, they negate the depth of the racial divide.

As if by being color-blind they can resolve the racial pain people of color live out. It is the inability to be open to the possibility that the experience of the other could be valid is a consistent element of white supremacy.

2. Shame and Hurt:

"I'm so embarrassed I said that!"

When focus remains on the white person and their emotional wounds this is classic deflection and redirection.

This common phrase can be heard when something hurtful may have been said to a person of color. The truly injured party, however, remains unrecognized. By having the courage to confront a racial slight, a person of color is made to feel that they have misread white people, or hurt their feelings.

They might also say: *I'm hurt that you think of me like that.* This further draws the attention back to them, and away from the real issue of pain felt by the person of color. When sympathy transfers to the white person no awareness or learning occurs. No trust is built.

3. Narcolepsy and Ignorance:

Shutting down or going blank is referred to as *race-related narcolepsy*. Racism retains a foothold when white people reach a threshold in their racial sensitivity and invoke their white privilege to *check out* and go silent, instead of sticking out the racial awareness process. The other side of that coin is simply to choose ignorance. *I had no idea about that!*

You're feeling of being clueless leads to detachment. The responsibility to look inward is traded for making the person of color assume the responsibility for bringing cultural and racial awareness to the surface.

4. Masochism:

When a white liberal's guilt runs amuck, it may become a deep seated need to take his or her racial lumps. Taking the neighborhood's homeless black man in for a meal may help him but does the giving come from a place of joy or guilt? What happens when he steals from you? In retrospect, was your original act helpful or masochistic? Perhaps a $10 dona-tion on the street might have served both of you better. White liberals who unconsciously seek self-punishment for historical oppression appear racially sensitive but they actually perpctuate racism by simply becoming a receptacle for poten-tial and actual abuse instead of examining their racially biased behavior.

5. Apology and Fake Compassion:

"I'm so sorry. I feel your pain."

This is an example of a deflective technique many white people use to draw attention away from an initial biased encounter. Again, not taking time to look inward stops short of sincere sensitivity. While displaying empathy toward another is often associated with an act of connection the speed with which white people rush to express sympathy and understanding at the expense of acknowledging their participation in racist behavior and ideology discourages a deep relational connection in the moment.

6. Defensiveness:

"But you know me. I'm not a racist!"

This response to confrontation happens all the time. A white person reminds black people that they personally owned no slaves, their relative marched with Dr. King, and they were into NWA before they got big so obviously they're in the clear regarding racism. Defensiveness is intended to end the discussion, absolve him or her, and quiet accusations surrounding white privilege. You really just built a brick wall.

7. The Pain Game:

"You're not the only ones. My family was wiped out in the Holocaust."

These micro invalidations are meant to silence, diminish and denigrate the experience of the person of color. Comparisons made to other races or cultural groups are insensitive. Creating a contest of pain keeps racist language alive, highlights deep insensitivity and is yet another deflection from the initial micro invalidation that if explored, could be enlightening.

Some American Jews use this micro invalidation often, comparing slavery and 300 years of oppression to the Holocaust. This is not the bridge to connection as intended but rather brings the focus back to the white person, further invalidating the person of color.

8. Racial Resume:

"I voted for Obama!"

Many white liberals keep a mental, multicultural resume to be submitted as evidence of racial tolerance and support

However, talking about how we have black friends, coached an inner-city basketball team, or live in a racially mixed neighborhood does not excuse them from internal racial insensitivity. This micro invalidation denies the person of color their feelings because they then have to argue with white people's resumes.

9. White Guilt:

"I feel terrible about all the police brutality against black people."

A person experiencing white guilt will attempt to provide comfort as if to make up for the indignation expressed by the person of color.

They may want to *do the right thing* but because no real change or self-examination is engaged, no awareness takes place.

10. Intellectualization:

"But we have a black president!"

As a defensive tool, a white person might bring up societal exceptions and success stories to negate the experience of someone who challenges their racial biases.

These examples are held up as reasons why white people can dismiss the experience of the person of color: because logically, African Americans should not be having the experience they are having.

Some white liberals want to walk the walk but they have to do more. They have to acknowledge the uncomfortable value of political correctness as a change agent.

If you truly want a different world, ask yourselves:

– *Is it possible that you might unintentionally say something that might be perceived as invalidating by black people?*

– *Can you take an honest inventory of your unintentional micro invalidation if black people confront you? What is your go-to defense? Denial? Hurt? Fake Compassion, Pain Game, Intellectualization?*

– *Can you engage with African Americans without deferring to internal defenses, especially when your unintended micro invalidations and unconscious sense of superiority are confronted?*

– *Can you be open to the impact of your words, expressing interest and caring how one's actions have been perceived?*

– *Can you simply say:* **I wasn't aware that my words or actions hurt you. Tell me more so I can learn?**

What has become known as the "cult of individualism" has constructed people in the West in such a way that they find it very difficult to understand anything outside their own experience. They individualize situations rather than approach them with systemic analysis in mind (e.g., the preference for seeing racism as isolated, overt, or an extreme incident such as racial epithets, rather than an ongoing and often unintentional set of attitudes which lead to structures of domination). Individualism fosters a belief that everybody is free to choose, that their destiny is within their own control and that choice, determination, "pulling oneself up by one's boot straps," are all individually determined and ultimately achievable despite social, economic, racial and cultural circumstances.

These are tough questions. It hurts to know that words might have invalidated another and that you may have contributed to racism. Only through continued growth, awareness and acknowledgement that words matter can something as ugly as racism be overcome.

VIII.

Gentrification and the Destruction of the Black Community

Gentrification involves the transformation of under-invested, predominately poor communities from low value to high value. During this transformation, long-time residents and businesses are displaced; unable to afford higher rents, mortgages and property taxes. For some, gentrification is a process of renovating deteriorated urban neighborhoods through the influx of more affluent residents. To others, gentrification magnifies the racial divide as it shifts a neighborhood's racial composition as white residents move in and minorities are moved out. According to a 2015 governing survey, gentrification accelerated in several cities with nearly 20% of neighborhoods with lower incomes and home values experiencing gentrification since 2000. That's compared to only 9% during the 1990s. The causes of gentrification are debatable. Some suggest it is caused by social and cultural factors, including family structure, rapid job growth, and lack of housing, traffic congestion, and public-sector policies. According to the CDC, there are definite health impacts. Studies indicate that vulnerable populations typically have shorter life expectancy, higher cancer rates, more congenital disabilities, greater infant mortality and a higher incidence of asthma, diabetes, and cardiovascular disease.

Coined "Negro Removal" in the 1960's by James Baldwin, the process of gentrification can happen so gradually it appears to be a subtle phenomenon. To address gentrification, Marqueece Harris-Dawson, Los Angeles city council member (8th District), and congresswoman Karen Bass gathered local government officials and community and faith-based leaders for a discussion on the causes and responses to gentrification at the Congressional Black Caucus' 48th Annual Legislative Conference. The conversation included Nefertiti Jackmon, Executive Director, Six Square Austin's Black Cultural District; Tracey Ross, Associate Director of Policy Link, Mindy Fullilove, Clinical Psychiatrist and Author of *Root Shock: How Tearing Up City Neighborhoods Hurt America and What We Can Do About It,* and Ras Baraka, Mayor of Newark, New Jersey.

"It is inspiring to see the leadership on the panel committed to finding solutions," said Bass. "We need to build more coalitions of government, community, and academics to address this critical community issue. We studied the issue and we realized rapid displacement was happening in every big city across the country. I wanted to convene this discussion because this is a national crisis and we need a national discussion to identify concrete solutions," stated Harris-Dawson. Solutions like Destination Crenshaw, the first outdoor project of its kind in Los Angeles that uses an iconic city street name to provide the context for public artwork and design, will formally establish and memorialize an African American neighborhood to set the tone for community revitalization.

Gentrification has emerged as a major threat to African American communities that have been centers for black business/economic development, cultural and civic life for generations. Gentrification has become the watch-word for the displacement of African American culture. It is the *Negro Removal Program* of the 21st century.

There is an urgent need for people of African descent to mount a serious offensive to defend black communities from this insidious onslaught.

During the Civil Rights and Black Power movements, the term Negro Removal was virtually synonymous with urban renewal as local, state and federal highway development projects often disconnected and destroyed stable African American communities. It was not unusual for a local high-way project designed to benefit residents from the suburbs or a component of an interstate highway system to be routed through the center of a black community, uprooting and displacing black people or permanently weakening businesses, institutions, networks and relationships that bound folks together.

As advocates for black entrepreneurship correctly urge black people to create and support black business districts in our communities, it is useful to remember that urban renewal destroyed thriving business districts in black communities across the country in the latter part of the 20th century. In fact, there is a historical pattern of marginalizing, subverting and outright destroying black communities to thwart the ability to achieve full political and economic empowerment as well as equity in this nation. Gentrification is the latest manifestation of this pattern.

Black neighborhoods, once the domain of black political and economic power is vanishing as increasing numbers of whites who in previous generations abandoned urban centers for the suburbs are now returning to establish more comfortable and convenient spaces in closer proximity to their work places. Development to accommodate the newcomers is driving up the cost of housing, especially rental properties in a manner that is unaffordable for large numbers of black residents. Property taxes are also skyrocketing, putting enormous pressure on black homeowners as well. As African American are displaced and replaced by newcomers, this is inevitably leading to dramatic shifts in political power from neighborhood advisory boards to city councils and the offices of mayors. Black power is diminishing.

What is equally egregious are the attitudes of some of the newcomers, whom residents of black communities sometimes characterize as invaders or neo-colonialists. This is because some newcomers are not content to become a part of the community. They arrogantly attempt to change the rhythms, culture and character of the community. Let me say the obvious, any person in the United States has the freedom to live wherever they choose. People of African descent have waged a relentless struggle to achieve this precious right. People also have the right to live amongst their own nationality, ethnicity of ethnic group if they choose, hence there are Irish, Italian, Polish, German and Jewish communities in this country. And occasionally these communities change in composition. Little Italy in lower Manhattan is now mostly shops and stores as people of Italian descent have largely chosen to migrate to other neighborhoods. Voluntary migration is one thing, forced displacement is another matter.

Time and time again, African Americans have faced schemes, targeted policies and outright violence, (e.g., Tulsa and Rosewood) to force their removal from neighborhoods and communities they worked, invested in and developed as their home.

Black people believe in development and no reasonable person would be opposed to improvements or progress that would better their community. The crucial issue for people of African descent is not development, it is *development* that is displacing black people and the culture. Therefore, the order and challenge of the day is to achieve development without displacement.

Philadelphia for example, is among leaders in gentrification, which has pushed out people of color. "A major transformation is occurring in the most prosperous American cities," the authors of the study conducted by the National Community Reinvestment Coalition wrote, and that has disproportionately hurt African Americans and Latinos "who were pushed away before they could benefit from increased property values and opportunities in revitalized neighborhoods." In 2019, local studies have found that homeowners here are not as threatened by displacement as in other places, due to the emergence of programs aimed at keeping people in their houses, and to relatively low property taxes, at least as compared with other locales. But renters, who make up nearly half of all city residents, have faced an eviction crisis as neighborhood investment surges. The new study identified more than 1,000 neighborhoods in 935 cities and towns where gentrification took place between 2000 and 2013. Rapidly rising rents, property values, and taxes forced more than 135,000 residents to move out.

In Washington, D.C., 20,000 black residents were forced out, and in Portland, Ore., 13% of the African American community was displaced during a decade. Nearly 12,000 African Americans in Philadelphia moved out of gentrifying neighborhoods. The study, *Shifting Neighborhoods: Gentrification and Cultural Displacement in American Cities*, relied on Census Bureau and economic data. The authors said it lent weight to what critics describe as a concentration of wealth and wealth-building investment in a handful of the nation's biggest cities.

The question is can development strategies be devised that prioritize improving the lives of the current residents and preserving the culture and character of their communities? The answer to that question is yes. The collective brain-power, skill, experience and will exists within black America to mount an offensive to defend black communities against gentrification; the Negro Removal program of the 21st century. Therefore, we must gather our brightest and best, the conscious and committed in our brain trust to devise plans and a policy agenda to rescue and preserve black communities. We possess the collective genius to develop just, safe, viable, vibrant and sustainable black communities. Now is the time to act boldly and courageously to defend black communities from the destructive forces of gentrification.

IX.

The Crime Bill of 1994

2019 marked the 25th anniversary of the passage of the most sweeping crime bill in U.S. history – the Violent Crime Control and Law Enforcement Act of 1994, also known as the Crime Bill. In many ways, the 350-page bill's passage characterized the bipartisan tough-on-crime movement of the late 20th century. While the bill contained a handful of positive provisions such as increased accountability for law enforcement and new protections for survivors of domestic violence and sexual assault, it was also responsible for exacerbating racial disparities in criminal justice involvement.

The Center for American Progress work has pointed out that the bill contributed to the ongoing rampant police misconduct and racial profiling by deploying hundreds of thousands of officers into neighborhoods of color and it jeopardized reentry for returning people of color by eliminating their Pell Grant eligibility while in prison. The bill also expanded the use of the death penalty imposed mandatory life sentences for individuals with three or more felony convictions and levied harsh new penalties for justice-involved youth. Many of these harmful provisions remain in effect in 2020 and continue to target and destabilize communities of color. Here are three ways that the 1994 Crime Bill continues to undermine the safety and well-being of communities of color:

1. Authorized the death penalty for 60 new federal offenses

Known as a *direct descendant of lynching*, the death penalty has always targeted and terrorized African Americans and Latino communities. The Crime Bill's Federal Death Penalty Act permitted the use of the death penalty for 60 new federal offenses, including certain drug offences not related to a homicide. In the five years following the bill's passage, 74% of defendants with death penalty recommendations from federal prosecutors were people of color. Notably, 44% were African American and 21% were Hispanic.

Racial disparities in capital punishment persist in 2020. While African Americans and Hispanics represent just 31% of the U.S. population, they represent 53% of death row inmates. Furthermore, the death penalty is more likely to be recommended when the victim of the crime is white rather than black, despite the fact that black men are the most likely victims of homicide. In 2018, the Trump administration called upon federal prosecutors to pursue the death penalty in cases dealing in extremely large quantities of drugs. If this directive survives litigation, it is expected to worsen racial disparities in the application of the death penalty, as black people are far more likely than white people to be arrested, charged, convicted, and incarcerated for drug crimes even though they use and sell drugs at similar rates.

2. Imposed mandatory life sentences for individuals with three or more felony convictions

The Crime Bill implemented a rash of new three-strike laws; laws that impose automatic life sentences for people convicted of certain felony offenses if they already have two convictions on their record. Dozens of states followed suit and enacted three-strike laws, resulting in a ballooning of the incarceration rate in certain states, especially for African Americans and Latino Americans.

Imposing life sentences simply because an individual has a criminal record disproportionately targets people of color who are more likely to have a record in the first place because of unequal contact with police and the justice system. Harsh collateral consequences limit employment opportunities for returning citizens especially people of color and increase the likelihood of recidivism. The Crime Bill's three-strike provision sent thousands of Americans to prison for life based on previous offenses for minor crimes such as stealing loose change from a parked car. In 2016, 78.5% of Americans serving life sentences in federal prison were people of color.

Some states have recognized the damage and disproportionate effect that three-strikes sentencing has on communities of color, especially black communities and have undergone major reform efforts. In California, for instance, black people were 12 times more likely than white people to be incarcerated under the *Three-Strike* laws until the state passed the Three Strikes Reform Act of 2012. This act amended the law to require one's third strike to be a series or violent felony and allowed those currently serving three-strikes sentences to petition the courts for a reduction of their term. However, 28 states still have a three-strike sentence on the books. In Maryland, Mississippi, and Louisiana, black people alone constitute approximately three-quarters of those sentenced to life in prison. While the federal government recently replaced its mandatory life sentence with a 25 year minimum sentence, it neglected to apply this change retroactively, meaning that hundreds of African Americans will die in prison as a result of the three-strike law.

3. Levied harsh new penalties for justice involved youth

The Crime Bill also expanded the school-to-prison pipeline and increased racial disparities in juvenile justice involvement by creating draconian penalties for so-called super predators – low-income children of color, especially black children, who are convicted of multiple crimes. Among other things, the Crime Bill allowed prosecutors to charge 13-year-old children as adults for certain crimes. As a result, two-thirds of Americans who were sentenced to life in prison as juveniles are African Americans. Juveniles of color also constitute a majority of cases that are transferred to adult criminal court, regardless of the offense. Additionally, the bill included an increase in funding for school resource officers (SROs).

These school-based, licensed police officers can make arrests and are sometimes armed, depending on local jurisdictions. This increase exacerbated the school-to-prison pipeline for black children as SROs are twice as likely to discipline black students compared with white students. The bill also called for sentencing enhancements for youth who are convicted of certain offenses and believed to be associated with gangs. However, while white youth represent a significant portion of self-identified gang members, at 40%, law enforcement report that more than 90% of gang members are people of color. As a result, police and prosecutors are more likely to target people of color for suspected gang association.

Black Leaders Supported the Crime Bill of 1994:

It's an easy target to blame Bill Clinton and other white politicians for the passage of the Crime Bill of 1994 but African Americans leaders were split on the controversial proposals. Kurt Schmoke, the first elected African American mayor of Baltimore, encouraged community leaders to support the bill, insisting that they needed to "Send a signal that if there is evil manifested by actions taken by individuals who choose to prey upon our residents that the evil will be responded to quickly and correctly." Others were of a different mind. U.S. Representative Kweisi Mfume, chairman of the Congressional Black Caucus (CBC), complained that the measures would only, "Find better ways to incarcerate people and give us a sense that we are more secure as a result of the new prisons and the tougher sentences."

In general, the community embraced both social programs and punishment. In March 1994, Ebony Magazine published an editorial that referenced a 1979 special issue on *Black on Black Crime*. The piece quoted Ebony publisher John H. Johnson, who wrote at the time that, "Black on Black crime has reached a crime level that threatens our existence as a people." The African American magazine reaffirmed those words and the policy responses outlined in that issue including economic development and a crackdown on incorrigible criminals. Because the crime bill included funds for crime prevention and rehabilitation programs and for police and prisons, many black leaders rushed to its defense. Thirty-nine African American pastors signed a letter saying, "While we do not agree with every provision in the crime bill, we do believe and emphatically support the bill's goal to save our communities and most importantly, our children." Ten black, big city mayors sent a letter to Mfume urging the caucus to support the proposals despite its opposition to the death penalty provisions. Given the size of the group, the CBC was able to hold up the legislation. At first, they used that leverage to protest capital punishment. Eventually though, party ties outweighed principled objections. In fact, Mfume, once a critic, engineered a meeting between his members and President Clinton in order to corral votes from members of the black caucus. As Charlie Rangel recounted about the gathering, "Clinton was selling his presidency." And the pitch worked. Party loyalty won out. Most CBC members stood by their president and party voting for the bill and aiding its passage.

Although, some applauded black leaders' emphasis on reform, they must also reckon with their embrace of police and the expansion of prisons. We must confront the disturbing truth that many African American politicians rushed to aid Bill Clinton and guard the influence they had accrued during their party's control of Washington.

The ways in which the criminal justice system operates to disadvantage black people are systemic, ingrained, and often subtle. An evidence brief from the Vera Institute of Justice, *An Unjust Burden: The Disparate Treatment of Black Americans in the Criminal Justice System*, presents a summary of research demonstrating how America's history of racism and oppression continues to manifest in the criminal justice system and perpetuates the disparate treatment of black people. This evidence brief comes at a time when the conversation around our country's fraught history of violence and discrimination against African American communities continue to receive national attention.

"The racial disparities that exist at each and every juncture of the justice system are significant and indisputable. But the reasons behind these disparities are complex and demand deeper understanding" said Nicholas Turner, Executive Director of the Vera Institute of Justice. They are rooted in a history of oppression and discriminatory decision making that has deliberately targeted black people in a false and deceptive narrative of criminality in implicit as well as conscious bias and in the legacy of structural racism and segregation. We believe that society must reckon with the deep body of evidence of bias that has caused black communities to become over-incarcerated, over policed, impoverished and burdened with generational suffering.

Some findings described and contextualized in *An Unjust Burden* **include:**

- Bias by decision makers at all stages of the justice process disadvantages black people. Studies have found that they are more likely to be stopped by the police, detained pretrial, charged with more serious crimes and sentenced more harshly than white people. For example, a 2004 study found that when police officers were asked, *who looks criminal?* More often, police overwhelmingly chose black faces than white ones. Also, a 2013 study found that federal prosecutors are more likely to charge black people than similarly situated white people with offenses that carry higher mandatory minimum sentences.

- The notion of "black on black crime" has been invoked to counter #BlackLivesMatter protests of police shootings of black men, women and children by suggesting that the actual problem is black men shooting each other is not borne out by statistics. A report from the Bureau of Justice Statistics found that most violence occurs between victims and offenders of the same race, regardless of race. The rate of both black-on-black and white-on-white non-fatal violence declined 79% between 1993 and 2015.

- The number of homicides involving both a black victim and black perpetrator fell from 7,361 in 1991 to 2,570 in 2016.

- Living in poor communities exposes people to risk factors for both offending and arrest, as well as a history of structural racism, inequality of opportunity including de-industrialization, red-lining, and white flight from neighborhoods meant that black people are more likely to be living in such conditions of concentrated poverty. Twenty two percent of black people lived in poverty in 2016, compared to approximately 9% of white people. The widening reach of the criminal justice system in low-income communities of color further depletes resources and social capital in these places, perpetuating a tenacious cycle of poverty and criminal justice involvement.

- Discriminatory criminal justice policies and practices have historically and unjustifiably targeted black people since the Reconstruction Era to capitalize on a loophole in the 13th Amendment that states, "Citizens cannot be enslaved unless convicted of a crime." Black Codes, vagrancy laws, and convict leasing were all used to continue post-slavery control over newly freed people. The high arrest and incarceration rates of black Americans based on these racist policies deeply informed national discussions about racial differences that continue in 2020. A 2010 study found that white Americans overestimate the share of burglaries, illegal drug sales, and juvenile crime committed by black people between 20% - 30%.

- Discrimination continues in 2020 but in less overt ways, including through disparity in the enforcement of seemingly race-neutral laws. The *War on Drugs* for example, inspired policies like drug-free zones and habitual offender laws that produced differential outcomes by race. In Massachusetts, a 2004 review of sentencing data showed that African Americans and Latino accounted for 80% of drug-free zone convictions, even though 45% of those arrested statewide for drug offenses were white.

Conversely, the legacy of the Violent Crime Control and Law Enforcement Act, aka the Crime Bill of 1994 continues to harm communities of color in 2020. It is past time for lawmakers to dismantle these harmful policies and enact comprehensive public safety solutions that reduce reliance on incarceration, prevent unnecessary criminalization, and eliminate the draconian laws keeping millions of Americans in prison. Further, racism in the criminal justice system is inherent and undeniable and this analysis highlights why disproportionate numbers of African Americans and people of color are behind bars in 2020.

X.

Assault on the Black Family

Millions of Americans form their opinions of African American families through the media's disturbing and inaccurate portrayal of black communities. The current media landscape is shaped by decision makers who continue to inaccurately depict black fathers as absent, black mothers as bad decision makers and African American families as destabilizing forces in society. We see these distortions and inaccuracies not only in right-wing outlets like Breitbart, but in unexpected places like the New York Times and Meet the Press and they have grave consequences. Not only are these systemic patterns in news coverage simply inaccurate, they also harm American families by justifying federal and state policies that will doom African American families for generations to come.

News and opinion media continue to reinforce the unfounded and unfair idea that black families are sources of personal, cultural and societal instability and that they are responsible for poverty, welfare and crime, rather than those who shape the economic and social environment families live in. It is not just the glut of negative representations that hurt black families but it is also the absence of positive ones. This is even more striking if you consider how consistently news and opinion media advance white families as models of social stability. These portrayals reinforce the implicit bias people already have about racial difference which inform behaviors and attitudes that show up in all aspects of our lives including at the voting booth.

In a report by the Color of Change entitled, *Family Story* laid out recommendations for how media outlets can begin addressing their inaccurate and harmful portrayals of African American families. Media outlets must stop propagating negative stereotypes of African Americans that do not have basis in fact.

- Media outlets must revise their standards and protocols for reporting on African American families and race-related issues.

- Media outlets must educate editorial decision makers and reporters about commonly spreading misinformation and stereotyping in reporting of African Americans.

- Media outlets must include people of color in the editorial process.

Further, scholar Travis L. Dixon penned an article entitled, *A Dangerous Distortion of Our Families: Representation of Families, By Race in News and Opinion Media.* Dixon penned the article based on his analysis of 200 television, print and online news stories produced between January 2015 and December 2016. His findings highlight the extent to which news media misrepresent African American parents and children as pathologically corrupt and violent. Color of Change executive director Rashad Robinson argued in the report's foreword that, "These racist media frames contribute to destructive perceptions about African American families."

"The current media landscape is shaped by decision makers who continue to inaccurately depict black fathers as absent, black mothers as bad decision makers and black families as de-stabilizing forces in society," Robinson wrote. We see these distortions and inaccuracies not only in right-wing outlets like Breitbart, but in unexpected places like The New York Times and Meet the Press – and they have grave consequences. Not only are these systemic patterns in news coverage simply inaccurate but they also harm American families by justifying federal and state policies that will doom African American families for generations to come.

These three key findings illuminate the extent of this misrepresentation using statistics pulled from the report:

1.) **News coverage portrays 59% of families living below the federal poverty line as African American.**

This stands in contrast with the 27% of black families actually living in poverty. The same media portrays only 16% of white families that way when in fact they represent 66% of impoverished Americans.

2.) **Media outlets depict 60% of African Americans families as welfare recipients.**

Black families make up 42% of the country's welfare recipients but receive disproportionate attention from publications that connect welfare to entitlement and laziness. That coverage also rarely acknowledges the history of economic segregation that impacts black communities into the present. White families make up 22% of welfare recipients and represent a near-proportional 23% of the beneficiaries portrayed in the news.

3.) **Unverified myths of black absentee fathers persist and news media characterizes 60% of African American fathers as abandoning their children.**

That's three times as much as absentee white fathers (20%) depicted in the media.

During the past 30 years, well over a thousand publications have been added to the research record on African American families in the United States. The count would be much higher if we adopted a broader interpretation of what qualifies as systematic, scientific study of African American families. To do so would require the inclusion of additional sources from a wide range of scholarly, literary, popular, and religious writings. Despite the voluminous research on black family life, scholars in this area are still uneasy. This uneasiness is caused by continued negative references to the African American family.

Such references ignore the extensive regional, ethnic, value, and income differences among African American families. It is an uneasiness with the theoretical and methodological shoddiness, bordering on suspension of the scientific method, apparent in so many published, widely circulated studies of African American families. This uneasiness is bred by entrenched, stereotypic portrayals of African American family life that not only persist but dominate. It is an uneasiness due to a frequently demonstrated ignorance concerning the internal dynamics and motives of African American family life in this society.

Much that is written about African American families is flawed by the tendency of researchers to gloss over within group differences. While prior research has explored African American/White family differences, information is relatively sparse regarding differences among African American families of different incomes, regions, life cycle stages, and value orientations. As a result, monolithic, stereotypic characterizations of African American families abound. The African American family headed by a single mother with numerous children and living in a roach infested tenement is a familiar stereotype. This image has been reinforced in the hallowed halls of universities, on the frenetic sets of movie and television shows, as well as in the halls of Congress. This stereotype represents but a limited slice of African American family life in the United States and it distorts the truth about female headed households in the black community. Such stereotypes leave the genuinely curious searching for the true face(s) of African American family life in this country. As a society, the United States is comfortable with stereotypes. Indeed, we revel in them. Stereotypes serve a useful function: *they help reduce the complexity, nuances, and dilemmas of life to manageable proportions.* In this respect, Americans are no different from other people. Generally speaking, humans seek to organize reality by extracting neat categories of meaning(s). Thus, we become accustomed to lose usage of terms charged with unstated implications in order to summarize our day-to-day experiences.

Race is an area of inquiry in the social and behavioral sciences that is particularly affected by our willingness to accept simplistic, unsupported, and stereotypic statements at face value. Such scientific confusion may have complex explanations such as the difficulty of disentangling race from culture, from history or the explanations may be simpler as in the failure to recognize that race is not a perfect predictor of a person's psyche, values, or even experiences. Therefore, for both complex and simple reasons, race continues to be one of the most widely studied, yet most poorly understood areas of scientific inquiry. How we think about and interact around race, therefore, exerts profound influence on the broader realities of individuals, groups, and institutions who are African American. These are topics requiring further study.

Predictably, African American family studies share many problems with the related area of race relations research. Writers in the area obscure much of the richness, complexity, and subtleties of African American family systems through their use of crude categories, poorly defined concepts, and negative stereotypes. Apparent in the literature are abundant references to *family disorganization*, the *underclass*, *culture of poverty*, and the *black matriarchy*. Such terms are offered, picked up, and repeated as if they effectively summarized the reality of African American family life in this society.

Consequently, with successive repetition, such concepts and the myths that they represent become more palatable and more believable. Equally dissatisfying are terms offered from the *other side* in the ongoing debate over pathology and well-being among African American families.

XI.

Reparations for African Americans: Redemption for the Soul of America

A bill calling for the federal government to study and consider how to provide reparations to African Americans for slavery has been introduced into every session of the US Congress for the last thirty years. The bill's aim is to *address the fundamental injustice, cruelty, brutality, and inhumanity of slavery in the United States and the thirteen American colonies between 1619 and 1865.* Former Representative John Conyers, the primary sponsor of the bill stated in 2017 just before he retired from the Congress, "I'm not giving up. Slavery is a blemish on this nation's history and until it is formally addressed, our country's story will remain marked by this blight." Through both Democratic and Republican control of the House, the bill only once got a hearing (2007) but possibly again in 2020, since House Speaker Nancy Pelosi voiced support for the proposal.

In 2019, three former Democratic presidential candidates: Kamala Harris, Elizabeth Warren, and Julián Castro endorsed the concept of granting reparations to African Americans affected by slavery and racial discrimination. By contrast, Senator Bernie Sanders decried the call for reparations as, "Divisive." David Brooks made the case for reparations on the editorial page of The New York Times and Ta-Nehisi Coates's foundational essay on reparations from 2014's publication in the Atlantic magazine received renewed interest. It seems that the time for meaningful consideration of reparations for slavery may have finally arrived – 154 years after the institution of slavery was formally abolished in the United States.

The ripening of this realization has emerged as a response to the intractability of African Americans' second-class political status in the US and the undeniable historical roots of black poverty, including data (2018) from the Federal Reserve's Survey of Consumer Finances showing that the typical African American family has only ten cents for every dollar of wealth held by the typical white family. There is a ready and workable model of how to repair the intergenerational disadvantage suffered by black people in the U.S. In communities across the country, racial justice activists have developed creative legal measures to move control and ownership of land into African American communities. A collective, land-based approach to reparations makes particular sense as a remedy to redress the dire injustice suffered by humans who were treated as property.

Today's emerging embrace of the moral imperative of granting reparations for slavery to black people renews an unanswered call that dates back to the end of the Civil War. There was then a widely accepted notion that delivering justice to formerly enslaved people must entail something more than emancipation alone. Contemporary calls for reparations premised on the notion that the past has enduring moral and material relevance today. Slavery, though outlawed has an enduring afterlife that pervades American culture and that we should face and make amends from its insufferable past.

In fact, Union military and political leaders who were directly responsible for stewarding African Americans from enslavement into their new lives as freed people felt strongly that slavery was an atrocity and a theft that required compensation. Reparations were understood as both a remedy for the rape, torture, death, and destruction of millions of human souls and a measure that recognized that freedom without material resources would lock black people into second-class status for generations to come. And it did. Land-based reparations were thus promised at the end of the Civil War with ambitious programs undertaken in several significant communities in the south. In the Sea Islands off South Carolina, and on the plantations owned by slaveholders and Confederate President Jefferson Davis and his brother Joseph just outside of Vicksburg, Mississippi, radical experiments in-land redistribution to formerly enslaved people were undertaken explicitly as a form of reparation for slavery.

Indeed, the process of redistributive justice began well before the war was over, as early as 1861. On November 3 of that year, the largest attack fleet ever to sail under the US flag was amassed to capture Port Royal, South Carolina. Confederate white islanders were clearly outgunned and outmanned, and three days later, nearly all of the local white men had packed their wives, children, and *favorite servants* (the innocuous term many slaveholders used for the people they enslaved) into boats and rowed to the mainland. Here, as elsewhere in the south, federal troops immediately emancipated black people held in bondage in territory under northern military control. So, when federal troops assumed control of the Sea Islands, approximately 10,000 black people living on 189 plantations were immediately set free; more than a year before President Lincoln issued the Emancipation Proclamation. Thus, began a huge project of allocating to free people land that had been confiscated by the federal government from Confederate plantation owners who fled the Sea Islands and abandoned their property. The enterprise of providing such reparations in the form of land titles became official policy when, in January 1865, Union General William Tecumseh Sherman issued Special Field Order No. 15, confiscating a strip of coastline stretching from Charleston, South Carolina to the St. John's River in Florida and into the mainland, thirty miles from the coast. The order redistributed the roughly 400,000 acres of land to newly freed black families in forty-acre lots. On this land, Sherman ordered, "No white person, unless military officers and soldiers detailed for duty will be permitted to reside and the freed people would be left to their own control."

Four months later, Confederate General Robert E. Lee surrendered to General Ulysses S. Grant at Appomattox. The daunting project of repairing the wounds of slavery through the issuance of *Sherman land titles* to the newly freed slaves continued, as did auctions of confiscated land in which freed people were able to purchase the land on which they had been enslaved. These original land titles are housed in the National Archives where freed people signed applications for land on which they and their people had not long before, been enslaved. Next to the *x* for many freed people's signatures are ink smudges appearing to bear witness to the trembling hands undertaking this remarkable act of freedom.

In this respect, the enslavement of black people which was a consequence of the overarching ideology of white supremacy was integral to America's national story and development as a nation. White supremacy metastasized from the original laws and customs that supported the enslavement of black people into so-called *Black Codes* that secured their subordinate status after slavery was formally abolished by the Thirteenth Amendment and in the succession of Jim Crow laws that secured a separate and unequal status for African Americans on the books and in practice. This entire legacy continues to structure the US economy and political system in 2020.

The failure to deliver real economic justice to formerly enslaved people relegated black people to the status of permanent second class citizens, kept down by a range of government policies and practices. At the same time, through numerous public programs that occurred as far back as 1785, the US government gave land to white people in order to facilitate wealth accumulation for the nation and for its white citizens. Real estate investment has been the greatest wealth-generating machine in our nation's history, yet African Americans have been systematically locked out of the opportunity to buy in, sit tight, and get rich. The GI Bill underwrote segregated housing through discriminatory lending policies. For decades, realtors steered black buyers to black neighborhoods and whites to white neighborhoods, while local and federal governments invested in the infrastructure in white neighborhoods but systematically underinvested in black neighborhoods.

The return of reparations, defined as the effort to address the wrongs done to African Americans throughout U.S. history, to the political agenda might seem oddly timed because of the current preoccupation with turning back the clock in so many policy areas. But Patricia Cohen of the New York Times laid out a number of economic models that might be used to calculate the losses suffered by American slaves and their descendants as well as the various ways by which those losses might be compensated. There is good reason to focus on the economic side of this question since economic disadvantage is at the core of how African Americans suffered under slavery, segregation and their legacies. The problem is that ultimately the responses to these wrongs must be political and would have to gain the endorsement of Congress if they are going to have any traction.

We know this in part from the experience of Japanese-Americans. Those who were interned as enemies of the state during World War II waited more than 30 years before they received compensation for the wrong done to them. Congress created a commission of inquiry in 1980 to address the issues. On the basis of its recommendations, the Civil Liberties Act of 1988 provided $20,000 for each surviving internee as well as an official apology from the government. The legislation was designed specifically to ensure that other groups – African Americans in particular would not see the law as a precedent.

The situation of African Americans had been addressed in the Kerner Commission empaneled by President Lyndon Johnson in the aftermath of a number of major urban riots in the late 1960s. Memorably, the commission concluded that, "Our nation is moving toward two societies, one black, and one white separate and unequal, and that *white racism* was the cause." The commission recommended massive programs to attack the impoverishment of urban ghettos and to improve the well-being of the black population. But the recommendations got caught in the meat grinder of presidential politics and Johnson, who had done so much to improve the situation of black people up till that point, essentially ignored the findings. And since the Kerner Commission, no such major official effort has been mounted to understand and respond to the inequities suffered by African Americans.

But the idea of a national commission of inquiry remains crucial to rectifying these long-simmering injustices. Such a commission would help build public support for reparations by analyzing the origins, nature and causes of racial inequality in the United States. The country's best historians, sociologists, economists, and political scientists would have to be assembled for the job. They would have to inquire into disparities in health, longevity, educational attainment, wealth, wages, employment, rates of incarceration and much more. Then on the basis of such an inquiry, appropriate measures could be recommended to Congress.

Most non-African Americans oppose reparations and always have. But if it can be shown how and why African Americans have long experienced unfair treatment and outcomes, we might finally as a nation come to terms with our long national nightmare of racial inequality. Although that nightmare has its roots in slavery it has continued long after the death of the last slave. The fact that no slaves are still alive has often gotten in the way of lawsuits intended to address racial inequality since, according to the courts, only a living victim of the wrong in question can have purpose to bring a suit. But those denials miss the real point: *racial inequality, however far back its roots may lie, still plagues the country in 2020.*

Conversely, white people have been given opportunities to profit from booming real estate markets that excluded African Americans. Promises made to freed people in 1865 that they would receive land as reparations for their enslavement and the leg up they needed to start their lives anew were never honored. Despite the enthusiasm of some of the 2020 Democratic presidential hopefuls and the increased attention to the topic, there remain many doubters who would have to be persuaded before reparations could become reality. A commission of inquiry into historic inequalities is likely the best and most politically plausible way to address them. It worked for Japanese-Americans after being placed in internment camps during World War II and perhaps, it will for African Americans.

XII.

Final Thoughts

Since 2005, African Americans have accomplished a considerable amount in the United States. From sports, entertainment, law enforcement, politics, African Americans and other people of color continue to rewrite the American landscape. We continue to make great strides in a nation where there are still individuals and institutions that view African Americans as second class citizens and for others – not citizens at all. As an African American, I have faced a war on two fronts as I have dealt with racism, bigotry, nepotism and scorn from other ethnic groups and sometimes, from African Americans. We continue to do battle within our communities jockeying for position of power.

Though some will argue to the contrary, American society in the Obama, post-Obama era and now the Trump administration is not beyond race. In fact, the present century has shaped up to be complex concerning what was known in a bygone era of race relations. The shooting of unarmed African Americans, the proposed building of a border wall between the U.S. and Mexico, fraught discussions over immigration and the continued protests over Confederate flags, statues in many southern cities are issues that continue to spark debates, protests and other forms of activism concerning the status of African Americans in America. For some, 2020 presents shades of the 1960s when citizens of all diverse backgrounds and ethnicities took to the streets to remake the American landscape and foster social change.

The course of American racial and ethnic politics over the next twenty years will depend not only on dynamics within the African American community but also on relationships between African Americans and other ethnic groups. However, this is difficult to analyze. The key question within the black community involves the relationship between material success and attachment to the American political and judicial system. The ethnic relations will illuminate the complexity of ethnic and racial coalitions and of ethnicity related policy issues that will affect African American political behavior. What makes prediction so difficult is not that there are no clear patterns in both areas but the current patterns are highly politically charged and therefore, highly volatile and contingent on a lot of people choices.

XIII.

Sources

Gramlich, John, *From police to parole, black and white Americans differ widely in their views of criminal justice system* (May 2019)

Dolan, Eric, *Black Americans tend to be most upset by Black-on-Black crime, study finds* (May 2019)

Crawford, Christine M, *How Can We Break Mental Health Barriers in Communities of Color?* (January 2019)

Whitesides, John, *More Americans say race relations deteriorating.* (April 2017)

Lopez, German and **Zarracina, Javier,** *Study: black people are 7 times more likely than white people to be wrongly convicted of murder.* (March 2017)

The Sentencing Project, *Report to the United Nations on Racial Disparities in the U.S. Criminal Justice System.* (April 2018)

Lopez, German, *American policing is broken. Here's how to fix it. Step one: Police must admit there's a problem.* (September 2017)

Smiley Calvin and **Fakunle, Davis,** *from "brute" to "thug:" the demonization and criminalization of unarmed Black male victims in America.* (January 2017)

Kendi, Ibram, *It's Time for Police to Start Snitching: Communities of color are actually disproportionately likely to report crimes – it's police themselves who have maintained a corrosive culture of silence* (May 2018)

Glaude, Eddie, *Don't Let the Loud Bigots Distract You. America's Real Problem with Race Cuts Far Deeper.* (September 2018)

Covert, Byrce, *The Not-So-Subtle Racism of Trump-Era Welfare Reform.* (May 2018)

Washington, Jessie, *African-Americans see painful truths in Trump victory.* (November 2016)

Otukoya, Debra, *What Characteristics Make You Black?* (January 2018)

Donaldson, Leigh, *When the media misrepresents black men, the effects is felt in the real world* (August 2015)

Kell, Gretchen, *Media is much to blame for negative stereotypes about African American men* (April 1997)

Mohdin, Aamna, *The media ends up racializing poverty by presenting a distorted image of black families* (December 2017)

Kimberly, Margaret, *Gentrification and the Death of Black Communities.* (May 2015)

Daniels, Dr. Ron, *Gentrification: The New Negro Removal Program: Displacing Black People and Culture.* (December 2018)

Vera Institute of Justice, *Research Confirms that Entrenched Racism Manifests in Disparate Treatment of Black Americans in the Criminal Justice System* (May 2018)

Fortner, Michael, *The Clintons Aren't the Only Ones to Blame for the Crime Bill: Black leaders also embraced it.* (October 2015)

Allen, Walter, *African American Family Life in Societal Context: Crisis and Hope* (July 2008)

Coates, Ta-Nehisi, *The Black Family in the Age of Mass Incarceration* (October 2015)

Dixon, Dr. Travis, *News Media Spreads Myths about Black Families* (December 2017)

Franke, Katherine, *Making Good on the Broken Promise of Reparations* (March 2019)

Clinton, Hillary, *Race and Repentance in America* (September 2018)

Hochschild, Jennifer L, *American Racial and Ethnic Politics in the 21st Century: A cautious look ahead* (March 1998)

Golan-Vilella, Marina, *Why SNAP Matters for Formerly Incarcerated People* (June 2018)

www.ingramcontent.com/pod-product-compliance
Lightning Source LLC
Chambersburg PA
CBHW020516290526
45786CB00002B/624